IN PARENTHESIS

IN PARENTHESIS

seinnyessit e gledyf ym

penn mameu

DAVID JONES

faber and faber

LONDON · BOSTON

First published in 1937
by Faber and Faber Limited
3 Queen Square London WC1N 3AU
First published in this edition 1963

Printed in England by Clays Ltd, St Ives plc
All rights reserved

Introduction © 1961 by T. S. Eliot

Publishers' note

For the 1978 impression a few corrections were
made to the text, following information given by David
Jones before his death to Professor William Blissett of
the University of Toronto.

A CIP record for this book is available
from the British Library

ISBN 0 571 05661 X

CONTENTS

A Note of Introduction

by T. S. Eliot

In Parenthesis was first published in London in 1937. I am proud to share the responsibility for that first publication. On reading the book in typescript I was deeply moved. I then regarded it, and I still regard it, as a work of genius.

A work of literary art which uses the language in a new way or for a new purpose, does not call for many words from the introducer. All that one can say amounts only to pointing towards the book, and affirming its importance and permanence as a work of art. The aim of the introducer should be to arouse the curiosity of a possible new reader. To attempt to explain, in such a note as this, is futile. Here is a book about the experiences of one soldier in the War of 1914-18. It is also a book about War, and about many other things also, such as Roman Britain, the Arthurian Legend, and divers matters which are given association by the mind of the writer. And as for the writer himself, he is a Londoner of Welsh and English descent. He is decidedly a Briton. He is also a Roman Catholic, and he is a painter who has painted some beautiful pictures and designed some beautiful lettering. All these facts about him are important. Some of them appear in his own Preface to this book; some the reader may discover in the course of reading.

When *In Parenthesis* is widely enough known—as it will be in time—it will no doubt undergo the same sort of detective analysis and exegesis as the later work of James Joyce and the *Cantos* of Ezra Pound. It is true that *In Parenthesis* and David Jones's later and equally remarkable work *The Anathemata*, are provided by the author with notes; but author's notes (as is illustrated by *The Waste Land*) are no prophylactic against interpretation and dissection: they merely provide the serious researcher with more material to interpret and dissect. The work of David Jones has some affinity with that of James Joyce (both men seem to me to have the Celtic ear for the music of words) and with the later work of Ezra Pound, and with my own. I stress the affinity, as any possible influence seems to me slight and of no importance. David Jones is a representative of the same literary generation as Joyce and Pound and myself, if four men born between 1882 and 1895 can be regarded as of the same literary generation. David Jones is the youngest, and the tardiest to publish. The lives of all of us were altered by that War, but David Jones is the only one to have fought in it.

Those who read *In Parenthesis* for the first time, need to know nothing more than this and what the author tells us in his own Preface, except that *In Parenthesis* and *The Anathemata* have been greatly admired by a number of writers whose opinions usually command attention. The commentaries, as I have said, will follow in time. Good commentaries can be very helpful: but to study even the best commentary on a work of literary art is likely to be a waste of time unless we have first read and been excited by the text commented upon even without understanding it. For that thrill of excitement from our first reading of a work of creative literature which we do not understand is itself the beginning of understanding, and if *In Parenthesis* does not excite us before we have understood it, no commentary will reveal to us its secret. And the second step is to get used to the book, to live with it and make it familiar to us. Understanding begins in the sensibility: we must have the experience before we attempt to explore the sources of the work itself.

PREFACE

This writing has to do with some things I saw, felt, & was part of. The period covered begins early in December 1915 and ends early in July 1916. The first date corresponds to my going to France. The latter roughly marks a change in the character of our lives in the Infantry on the West Front. From then onward things hardened into a more relentless, mechanical affair, took on a more sinister aspect. The wholesale slaughter of the later years, the conscripted levies filling the gaps in every file of four, knocked the bottom out of the intimate, continuing, domestic life of small contingents of men, within whose structure Roland could find, and, for a reasonable while, enjoy, his Oliver. In the earlier months there was a certain attractive amateurishness, and elbow-room for idiosyncrasy that connected one with a less exacting past. The period of the individual rifle-man, of the 'old sweat' of the Boer campaign, the 'Bairnsfather' war, seemed to terminate with the Somme battle. There were, of course, glimpses of it long after — all through in fact — but it seemed never quite the same. The *We've Lived and Loved Together* of the Devons was well enough for the Peninsula, but became meaningless when companion lives were at such short purchase. Just as now there are glimpses in our ways of another England—yet we know the truth. Even while we watch the boatman mending his sail, the petroleum is hurting the sea. So did we in 1916 sense a change. How impersonal did each new draft seem arriving each month, and all these new-fangled gadgets to master. Anyway, it is exclusively with the earlier period that this writing deals. Earlier still, before my participation, it must have been different again. None of the characters in this writing are real persons, nor is any sequence of events historically accurate. There are, I expect, minor anachronisms, e.g. the suggestion in Part 4 of a rather too fully developed gas-defence system for Christmas, 1915. The mention of 'toffee-apples' (a type of trench-mortar bomb so shaped) at perhaps too early a date. Each person

and every event are free reflections of people and things remembered, or projected from intimately known possibilities.
I have only tried to make a shape in words, using as data the
complex of sights, sounds, fears, hopes, apprehensions,
smells, things exterior and interior, the landscape and paraphernalia of that singular time and of those particular men.
I have attempted to appreciate some things, which, at the
time of suffering, the flesh was too weak to appraise. There
are passages which I would exclude, as not having the form
I desire — but they seem necessary to the understanding of
the whole.

My companions in the war were mostly Londoners with an
admixture of Welshmen, so that the mind and folk-life of those
two differing racial groups are an essential ingredient to my
theme. Nothing could be more representative. These came
from London. Those from Wales. Together they bore in their
bodies the genuine tradition of the Island of Britain, from Ben-
digeid Vran to Jingle and Marie Lloyd. These were the children of Doll Tearsheet. Those are before Caractacus was. Both
speak in parables, the wit of both is quick, both are natural
poets; yet no two groups could well be more dissimilar. It
was curious to know them harnessed together, and together
caught in the toils of 'good order and military discipline'; to
see them shape together to the remains of an antique regimental tradition, to see them react to the few things that united
us—the same jargon, the same prejudice against 'other arms'
and against the Staff, the same discomforts, the same grievan-
ces, the same maims, the same deep fears, the same pathetic
jokes; to watch them, oneself part of them, respond to the
war landscape; for I think the day by day in the Waste Land,
the sudden violences and the long stillnesses, the sharp contours and unformed voids of that mysterious existence, pro-
foundly affected the imaginations of those who suffered it. It
was a place of enchantment. It is perhaps best described in

Malory, book iv, chapter 15—that landscape spoke 'with a grimly voice'.

I suppose at no time did one so much live with a consciousness of the past, the very remote, and the more immediate and trivial past, both superficially and more subtly. No one, I suppose, however much not given to association, could see infantry in tin-hats, with ground-sheets over their shoulders, with sharpened pine-stakes in their hands, and not recall

> '. . . or may we cram,
> Within this wooden O . . .'

But there were deeper complexities of sight and sound to make ever present

> 'the pibble pabble in Pompey's camp'

Every man's speech and habit of mind were a perpetual showing: now of Napier's expedition, now of the Legions at the Wall, now of 'train-band captain', now of Jack Cade, of John Ball, of the commons in arms. Now of *High Germany*, of *Dolly Gray*, of Bullcalf, Wart and Poins; of Jingo largenesses, of things as small as the Kingdom of Elmet; of Wellington's raw shire recruits, of ancient border antipathies, of our contemporary, less intimate, larger unities, of *John Barleycorn*, of 'sweet Sally Frampton'. Now of Coel Hên—of the Celtic cycle that lies, a subterranean influence as a deep water troubling, under every tump in this Island, like Merlin complaining under his big rock.

It may be well to say something of the punctuation. I frequently rely on a pause at the end of a line to aid the sense and form. A new line, which the typography would not otherwise demand, is used to indicate some change, inflexion, or emphasis. I have tried to indicate the sound of certain sentences by giving a bare hint of who is speaking, of the influences operating to make the particular sound I want in a particular instance, by perhaps altering a single vowel in one word. I have only used the notes of exclamation, interrogation, etc., when

PREFACE

the omission of such signs would completely obscure the sense.
I hope the stresses and changes intended will convey themselves to the reader. I have been hampered by the convention
of not using impious and impolite words, because the whole
shape of our discourse was conditioned by the use of such
words. The very repetition of them made them seem litur-
gical, certainly deprived them of malice, and occasionally,
when skilfully disposed, and used according to established
but flexible tradition, gave a kind of significance, and even at
moments a dignity, to our speech. Sometimes their juxtapos-
ition in a sentence, and when expressed under poignant circumstances, reached real poetry. Because of publication, it
has been necessary to consider conventional susceptibilities.
Some such expressions have nevertheless of necessity become
part of the form this writing has taken. Quite obviously they
do not constitute blasphemy in any theological sense, and
that is all I would consider. Private X's tirade of oaths means
no more than 'I do not like this Vale of Tears'; whereas
Flossie's 'O, bother!' would waste a countryside had she an
efficacious formula. I say more: the 'Bugger! Bugger!' of a man
detailed, had often about it the 'Fiat! Fiat!' of the Saints.

I am surprised to find how much Cockney influences have
determined the form; but as Latin is to the Church, so is Cockney to the Army, no matter what name the regiment bears. It
is difficult to dissociate any word of command, any monosyl-
lable remembered, coming at you on dark duck-board track,
from the Great Bell of Bow. If the language of England passed
and all we know dissolved, some squad of savages, speaking a
new tongue, might yet respond to a sharp formula, remembered, fossilised: 'Kipt thet dressin cahncher', might well be
for them what *Kyrie Eleison* is, breaking the Latin crust, for
Father O'Connor's boy.

I did not intend this as a 'War Book'—it happens to be concerned with war. I should prefer it to be about a good kind of

xii

peace—but as Mandeville says, 'Of Paradys ne can I not speken propurly I was not there; it is fer beyonde and that for thinketh me. And also I was not worthi.' We find ourselves privates in foot regiments. We search how we may see formal goodness in a life singularly inimical, hateful, to us.

We are shy when pious men write A.M.D.G. on their notepaper — however, in the Welsh Codes of Court Procedure the Bard of the Household is instructed to sing to the Queen when she goes to her chamber to rest. He is instructed to sing first to her a song in honour of God. He must then sing the song of the Battle of Camlann—the song of treachery and of the undoing of all things; and afterward he must sing any song she may choose to hear. I have tried, to so make this writing for anyone who would care to play Welsh Queen.

I had intended to engrave some illustrations, but have been prevented.

I would say something of the 'Welsh' element. Ladely Worm, Brunanburh, Fair Worcester City, Fair Maid of Kent: these, rightly, for our ears, discover a whole English complex; whereas the Boar Trwyth, Badon Hill, Troy Novaunt, Elen of the Hosts, will only find response in those who, by blood or inclination, feel a kinship with the more venerable culture in that hotch-potch which is ourselves. Yet that elder element is integral to our tradition. From Layamon to Blake 'Sabrina' would call up spirits rather than 'Ypwines floet'. As Mr. Christopher Dawson has written: 'And if Professor Collingwood is right, and it is the conservatism and loyalty to lost causes of Western Britain that has given our national tradition its distinctive character, then perhaps the middle ages were not far wrong in choosing Arthur, rather than Alfred or Edmund or Harold, as the central figure of the national heroic legend.'[1]

[1] See *The Tablet*, December 5th, 1936. Mr. Dawson's review of *Roman Britain and the English Settlements*. R. G. Collingwood and J. N. L. Myres.

PREFACE

I would ask the reader to consult the notes with the text, as I regard some of them as integral to it.

One other thing. It is not easy in considering a trench-mortar barrage to give praise for the action proper to chemicals —full though it may be of beauty. We feel a rubicon has been passed between striking with a hand weapon as men used to do and loosing poison from the sky as we do ourselves. We doubt the decency of our own inventions, and are certainly in terror of their possibilities. That our culture has accelerated every line of advance into the territory of physical science is well appreciated—but not so well understood are the unforeseen, subsidiary effects of this achievement. We stroke cats, pluck flowers, tie ribands, assist at the manual acts of religion, make some kind of love, write poems, paint pictures, are generally at one with that creaturely world inherited from our remote beginnings. Our perception of many things is heightened and clarified. Yet must we do gas-drill, be attuned to many newfangled technicalities, respond to increasingly exacting mechanical devices; some fascinating and compelling, others sinister in the extreme; all requiring a new and strange direction of the mind, a new sensitivity certainly, but at a considerable cost.

We who are of the same world of sense with hairy ass and furry wolf and who presume to other and more radiant affinities, are finding it difficult, as yet, to recognise these creatures of chemicals as true extensions of ourselves, that we may feel for them a native affection, which alone can make them magical for us. It would be interesting to know how we shall ennoble our new media as we have already ennobled and made significant our old—candle-light, fire-light, Cups, Wands and Swords, to choose at random.

Some of us ask ourselves if Mr. X adjusting his box-respirator can be equated with what the poet envisaged, in

'I saw young Harry with his beaver on.'

PREFACE

We are in no doubt at all but what Bardolph's marching kiss for Pistol's 'quondam Quickly' is an experience substantially the same as you and I suffered on Victoria platform. For the old authors there appears to have been no such dilemma—for them the embrace of battle seemed one with the embrace of lovers. For us it is different. There is no need to labour the point, nor enquire into the causes here. I only wish to record that for me such a dilemma exists, and that I have been particularly conscious of it during the making of this writing.

I wish to thank those friends who have helped me — one very especially — and another I will mention by name. I do not think I should have continued, especially through the earlier stages, had it not been for the sensitive enthusiasm and understanding of Mr. Harman Grisewood.

To any Welsh reader, I would say, what Michael Drayton, in a foreword to his *Poly-olbion*, says, speaking of Wales: 'if I have not done her right, the want is in my ability, not in my love.'

This writing is called 'In Parenthesis' because I have written it in a kind of space between—I don't know between quite what—but as you turn aside to do something; and because for us amateur soldiers (and especially for the writer, who was not only amateur, but grotesquely incompetent, a knocker-over of piles, a parade's despair) the war itself was a parenthesis — how glad we thought we were to step outside its brackets at the end of '18—and also because our curious type of existence here is altogether in parenthesis.

D. J.

PS. I find I have neglected one thing that I very much wanted to say. There is the debt I owe to the printer who will print this for me. He is more than an aid, he is a collaborator, and I know no one else so aware of both the nature of a writing and of how to print it.

1st March 1937

THIS WRITING IS FOR MY FRIENDS
IN MIND OF ALL COMMON & HIDDEN
MEN AND OF THE SECRET PRINCES
AND TO THE MEMORY OF THOSE
WITH ME IN THE COVERT AND IN
THE OPEN FROM THE BLACKWALL
THE BROADWAY THE CAUSEWAY
THE CUT THE FLATS THE LEVEL THE
ENVIRONS AND THOSE OTHERS
FROM TRAETH MAWR AND LONG
MOUNTAIN THE HENDREF AND YR
HAFOD THE PENTRE PANDY AND Y
DARREN THE MAELORS THE BOUNDARY
WALLS AND NO. 4 WORKING
ESPECIALLY PTE. R.A. LEWIS-GUNNER
FROM NEWPORT MONMOUTHSHIRE
KILLED IN ACTION IN THE BOE-
SINGHE SECTOR N.W. OF YPRES
SOME TIME IN THE WINTER 1916-17
AND TO THE BEARDED INFANTRY
WHO EXCHANGED THEIR LONG
LOAVES WITH US AT A SECTOR'S
BARRIER AND TO THE ENEMY
FRONT-FIGHTERS WHO SHARED OUR
PAINS AGAINST WHOM WE FOUND
OURSELVES BY MISADVENTURE

Evil betide me if I do not open the door to know if that is true which is said concerning it. So he opened the door . . . and when they had looked, they were conscious of all the evils they had ever sustained, and of all the friends and companions they had lost and of all the misery that had befallen them, as if all had happened in that very spot; . . . and because of their perturbation they could not rest.

PART 1

THE MANY MEN SO BEAUTIFUL

Men marched, they kept equal step . . .
Men marched, they had been nurtured together.

'49 Wyatt, 01549 Wyatt.

Coming sergeant.

Pick 'em up, pick 'em up—I 'll stalk within yer chamber.

Private Leg . . . sick.

Private Ball . . . absent.

'01 Ball, '01 Ball, Ball of No. 1.

Where 's Ball, 25201 Ball—you corporal,

Ball of your section.

Movement round and about the Commanding Officer.

Bugler, will you sound 'Orderly Sergeants'.

A hurrying of feet from three companies converging on the little group apart where on horses sit the central command. But from 'B' Company there is no such darting out. The Orderly Sergeant of 'B' is licking the stub end of his lead pencil; it divides a little his fairish moist moustache.

Heavily jolting and sideway jostling, the noise of liquid shaken in a small vessel by a regular jogging movement, a certain clinking ending in a shuffling of the feet sidelong—all clear and distinct in that silence peculiar to parade grounds and to refectories. The silence of a high order, full of peril in the breaking of it, like the coming on parade of John Ball.

He settles between numbers 4 and 5 of the rear rank. It is as ineffectual as the ostrich in her sand. Captain Gwynn does not turn or move or give any sign.

Have that man's name taken if you please, Mr. Jenkins.

Take that man's name, Sergeant Snell.

Take his name, corporal.

Take his name take his number—charge him—late on parade—the Battalion being paraded for overseas—warn him for Company Office.

Have you got his name Corporal Quilter.

Temporary unpaid Lance-Corporal Aneirin Merddyn Lewis had somewhere in his Welsh depths a remembrance

1

of the nature of man, of how a lance-corporal's stripe is but held vicariously and from on high, is of one texture with an eternal economy. He brings in a manner, baptism, and metaphysical order to the bankruptcy of the occasion.

'o1 Ball is it—there was a man in Bethesda late for the last bloody judgment.

Corporal Quilter on the other hand knew nothing of these things.

Private Ball's pack, ill adjusted and without form, hangs more heavily on his shoulder blades, a sense of ill-usage pervades him. He withdraws within himself to soothe himself —the inequity of those in high places is forgotten. From where he stood heavily, irksomely at ease, he could see, half-left between 7 and 8 of the front rank, the profile of Mr. Jenkins and the elegant cut of his war-time rig and his flax head held front; like San Romano's foreground squire, unhelmeted; but we don't have lances now nor banners nor trumpets. It pains the lips to think of bugles—and did they blow Defaulters on the Uccello horns.[2]

He put his right hand behind him to ease his pack, his cold knuckles find something metallic and colder.

No mess-tin cover.

Shining sanded mess-tin giving back the cold early light. *Improperly dressed, the Battalion being paraded for overseas.* His imaginings as to the precise relationship of this general indictment from the book to his own naked mess-tin were with suddenness and most imperatively impinged upon, as when an animal hunted, stopping in some ill-chosen covert to consider the wickedness of man, is started into fresh effort by the cry and breath of dogs dangerously and newly near. For the chief huntsman is winding his horn, the officer commanding is calling his Battalion by name—whose own the sheep are.

55th Battalion!

Fifty-fifth Bat-tal-i-on

'talion!!

From 'D' to 'A' his eyes knew that parade. He detected no movement. They were properly at ease.

Reverberation of that sudden command broke hollowly upon the emptied huts behind 'D' Company's rear platoons. They had only in them the rolled mattresses, the neatly piled bed-boards and the empty tea-buckets of the orderly-men, emptied of their last gun-fire.[3]

Stirrups taut and pressing upward in the midst of his saddle he continues the ritual words by virtue of which a regiment is moved in column of route:

. . . the Battalion will move in column of fours to the right—'A' Company—'A' Company leading.

Words lost, yet given continuity by that thinner command from in front of No. 1. Itself to be wholly swallowed up by the concerted movement of arms in which the spoken word effected what it signified.

'A' Company came to the slope, their files of four turn right. The complex of command and heel-iron turned confuse the morning air. The rigid structure of their lines knows a swift mobility, patterns differently for those sharp successive cries.

Mr. P. D. I. Jenkins who is twenty years old has now to do his business:

No. 7 Platoon—number seven.

number seven—right—by the right.

How they sway in the swing round for all this multiplicity of gear.

Keept'y'r dressing.

Sergeant Snell did his bit.

Corporal Quilter intones:

Dress to the right—no—other right.

Keep those slopes.

Keep those sections of four.
Pick those knees up.
Throw those chests out.
Hold those heads up.
Stop that talking.
Keep those chins in.
Left left lef'—lef' righ' lef'—you Private Ball it's you
I'v got me glad-eye on.

So they came outside the camp. The liturgy of a regiment
departing has been sung. Empty wet parade ground. A camp-
warden, some unfit men and other details loiter, dribble
away, shuffle off like men whose ship has sailed.

The long hutment lines stand. Not a soul. It rains harder:
torn felt lifts to the wind above Hut 10, Headquarter Company; urinal concrete echoes for a solitary whistler. Corrugated iron empty—no one. Chill gust slams the vacant
canteen door.

Miss Veronica Best who runs the hut for the bun-wallahs⁴
stretches on her palliasse, she's sleepy, she can hear the band:
We've got too many buns—and all those wads⁵—you knew
they were going—why did you order them—they won't be
in after rouse-parade even—they've gone.

Know they've gone—shut up—Jocks from Bardown
move in Monday. Violet turns to sleep again.

Horses' tails are rather good—and the way this one springs
from her groomed flanks.

He turns slightly in his saddle.

You may march at ease.

No one said march easy Private Ball, you're bleedin'
quick at some things ain't yer.

PART 1

The Squire from the Rout of San Romano smokes Mela-
chrino No. 9.

The men may march easy and smoke, Sergeant Snell.

Some like tight belts and some like loose belts—trussed-
up pockets—cigarettes in ammunition pouches—rifle-bolts,
webbing, buckles and rain—gotta light mate—give us a
match chum. How cold the morning is and blue, and how
mysterious in cupped hands glow the match-lights of a con-
course of men, moving so early in the morning.

The body of the high figure in front of the head of the
column seemed to change his position however so slightly.
It rains on the transparent talc of his map-case.

The Major's horse rubs noses with the horse of the su-
perior officer. Their docked manes brush each, as two
friends would meet. The dark horse snorts a little for the
pulling at her bridle rein.

In 'D' Company round the bend of the road in the half-
light is movement, like a train shunting, when the forward
coaches buffer the rear coaches back. The halt was unexpected. How heavy and how top-heavy is all this martial
panoply and how the ground seems to press upward to
afflict the feet.

The bastard's lost his way already.

Various messages are passed.

Some lean on their rifles as aged men do on sticks in stage-
plays. Some lean back with the muzzle of the rifle support-
ing the pack in the position of gentlewomen at field sports,
but not with so great assurance.

It's cold when you stop marching with all this weight
and icy down the back.

Battalion cyclists pass the length of the column. There is
fresh stir in 'A' Company.

Keep your column distance.

The regular rhythm of the march has re-established it-self.

The rain increases with the light and the weight increases with the rain. In all that long column in brand-new overseas boots weeping blisters stick to the hard wool of grey government socks.

I'm a bleedin' cripple already Corporal, confides a limp-ing child.

Kipt' that step there.

Keep that proper distance.

Keept' y'r siction o' four—can't fall out me little darlin'. Corporal Quilter subsides, he too retreats within himself, he has his private thoughts also.

It's a proper massacre of the innocents in a manner of speaking, no so-called seven ages o' man only this bastard military age.

Keep that step there.

Keep that section distance.

Hand us thet gas-pipe young Saunders—let's see you shape —you too, little Benjamin—hang him about like a goddam Chris'us tree—use his ample shoulders for an armoury-rack—it is his part to succour the lambs of the flock.

With some slackening of the rain the band had wiped their instruments. Broken catches on the wind-gust came shrilly back:

Of Hector and Lysander and such great names as these —the march proper to them.[6]

So they went most of that day and it rained with increasing vigour until night-fall. In the middle afternoon the outer parts of the town of embarkation were reached. They halted for a brief while; adjusted puttees, straightened caps, fastened undone buttons, tightened rifle-slings and attended each one to his own bedraggled and irregular condition. The band recommenced playing; and at the attention and in excellent step they passed through the suburbs, the town's centre, and so towards the docks. The people of that town did not acclaim them, nor stop about their business—for it was late in the second year.[7]

By some effort of a corporate will the soldierly bearing of the text books maintained itself through the town, but with a realisation of the considerable distance yet to be covered through miles of dock, their frailty reasserted itself—which slackening called for fresh effort from the Quilters and the Snells, but at this stage with a more persuasive intonation, with almost motherly concern.

Out of step and with a depressing raggedness of movement and rankling of tempers they covered another mile between dismal sheds, high and tarred. Here funnels and mastheads could be seen. Here the influence of the sea and of the tackle and ways of its people fell upon them. They revived somewhat, and for a while. Yet still these interminable ways between—these incessant halts at junctions. Once they about-turned. Embarkation officers, staff people of all kinds and people who looked as though they were in the Navy but who were not, consulted with the Battalion Commander. A few more halts, more passing of messages, —a further intensifying of their fatigue. The platoons of the leading company unexpectedly wheel. The spacious shed is open at either end, windy and comfortless. Multifarious accoutrements, metal and cloth and leather sink with the perspiring bodies to the concrete floor.

Certain less fortunate men were detailed for guard, John Ball amongst them. The others lay, where they first sank down, wet with rain and sweat. They smoked; they got very cold. They were given tins of bully beef and ration biscuits for the first time, and felt like real expeditionary soldiers. Sometime between midnight and 2 a.m. they were paraded. Slowly, and with every sort of hitch, platoon upon platoon formed single file and moved toward an invisible gangway. Each separate man found his own feet stepping in the darkness on an inclined plane, the smell and taste of salt and machinery, the texture of rope, and the glimmer of shielded light about him.

So without sound of farewell or acclamation, shrouded in a dense windy darkness, they set toward France. They stood close on deck and beneath deck, each man upholstered in his life-belt. From time to time a seaman would push between them about some duty belonging to his trade.

Under a high-slung arc-light whose cold clarity well displayed all their sea weariness, their long cramped-upness and fatigue, they stumblingly and one by one trickled from the ship on to French land. German prisoners in green tunics, made greener by the light, heavily unloading timber at a line of trucks—it still rained, and a bitter wind in from the sea.

A young man, comfortable in a short fleece jacket, stood smoking, immediately beneath the centre of the arc—he gave orders in a pleasant voice, that measured the leisure of his circumstances and his class. Men move to left and right within the orbit of the light, and away into the half darkness, undefined, beyond it.

'B' Company were conducted by a guide, through back ways between high shuttered buildings, to horse-stalls, where they slept. In the morning, they were given Field Service postcards—and sitting in the straw they crossed out what did not apply, and sent them to their mothers, to their sweethearts.

PART I

Toward evening on the same day they entrained in cattle trucks; and on the third day, which was a Sunday, sunny and cold, and French women in deep black were hurrying across flat land—they descended from their grimy, littered, limb restricting, slatted vehicles, and stretched and shivered at a siding. You feel exposed and apprehensive in this new world.

PART 2

CHAMBERS GO OFF, CORPORALS STAY

On Tuesday they put on their dark blue raiment;
On Wednesday they prepared their enamelled shields.

PART 2

In a place of scattered farms and the tranquillity of fields, in a rest area many miles this side of the trench system; a place unmolested and untouched so far, by the actual shock of men fighting. They did short route marches each day along winding ways saturated with continued rain. They did platoon-drill and arm-drill in soggy fields behind their billets.

They were given lectures on very wet days in the barn, with its great roof, sprung, upreaching, humane, and redolent of a vanished order. Lectures on military tactics that would be more or less commonly understood. Lectures on hygiene by the medical officer, who was popular, who glossed his technical discourses with every lewdness, whose heroism and humanity reached toward sanctity.

One day the Adjutant addressed them on the history of the Regiment. Lectures by the Bombing Officer: he sat in the straw, a mild young man, who told them lightly of the efficacy of his trade; he predicted an important future for the new Mills Mk. IV grenade, just on the market; he discussed the improvised jam-tins of the veterans, of the bombs of after the Marne, grenades of Loos and Laventie — he compared these elementary, amateurish, inefficiencies with the compact and supremely satisfactory invention of this Mr. Mills, to whom his country was so greatly indebted.

He took the names of all those men who professed efficiency on the cricket field—more particularly those who claimed to bowl effectively—and brushing away with his hand pieces of straw from his breeches, he sauntered off with his sections of grenades and fuses and explanatory diagrams of their mechanism stuffed into the pockets of his raincoat, like a departing commercial traveller.

They rested cosily at night in thick straw. They crowded together in the evening—hours full of confused talking; the

13

tiny room heavy with the haze of smoking, and humane
with the paraphernalia of any place of common gathering,
warm, within small walls.

Sitting at circular tables, sometime painted green or blue,
now greyed and spotted with rust, and on the marble flat
stains of sticky *grenadine*, grey tepid coffee in glass filmed
with condensation, sour beer thinned with tank-water, sour
red wine. Three weeks passed in this fashion.

A week before Christmas, Corps communicated with
Division. Men on horseback, of evident aloofness, were seen
going and coming about Battalion Headquarters. An auto-
mobile would throw high the surface slime of the pulpy
roads in the neighbourhood of Brigade, lessening the brief-
ness of rest between parades, for each marching platoon
as it passed. The air was full with rumour, fantastic and
credible.

Up the line on Thursday afternoon—Monday—Thursday
morning—Saturday night—back to the Base—back to England, back to England—another part of the field—Corporal
B. just said so—Signaller X heard the Captain of 'D'
talking to—talking to—they say at the Transport lines—
Tim Bolney the Brigade Linesman heard over the wire—
I met a Divisional Cyclist—cookhouse rumour—rumour
from the Quartermaster's stores.

I don't think there is much else, you Captain Gower, you
understand—yes 'A' move last—yes, well, that is all—
platoons will parade outside their billets at 6 o'clock—
companies should be on the road at 6.20, the Battalion must
be assembled at Z 19 a 2 3—there—by the brewery at 8.15
—to embus at 8.30.

Company Commanders left the conference and turned
reflectively to their lodgings, and to find their sergeant-
majors.

PART 2

Reveille at 4.30, number seven—4.30.

The Orderly Sergeant's head came and went at the small aperture in the large hung door—he fussily hurried to No. 6, his pencil behind his ear.

Corporals and lance-corporals flitted about farm out-buildings, and chicken scurried; a dog rose leisurely and stretched. Up to the hay loft to give some detail to the Lewis-gunners, across by the midden to the shed by the cow-stall, to detail a man for the stretcher-bearers and another as company runner. A third, caught accidentally, half way up a ladder, for sanitary fatigue; through the or-chard behind the cookhouse to break up a group furtively playing some card game—he heard the clink of coin—and send them, full of discontent, each one about some largely differing, but essential task.

Private Saunders with two others spent three hours carry-ing away and burning the company's accumulated rubbish, at an incinerator at the far corner of the field where they did arm-drill. He regarded the place with a certain wist-fulness, as he poked jagged twisted tins, and litter of all kinds into the smouldering heap; the freely drawn rectangle of sodden green with its willow boundaries called fami-liarly to him. After all, the last three weeks had not been too bad. Platoon drill was tiresome, but Mr. Jenkins was kind. He used to sit by the little stream where they got their washing-water, and look into it for long at a time without moving, whilst they smoked under the turnip-stack, with someone watching to see if anyone—the Adju-tant, or that shit Major Lillywhite, was anywhere about. All that was finished with anyway. The Line—going up the line—up the line tomorrow morning and the reveille so early. He hoped the cooks would light their fires in time. Moving into the line. It had all the unknownness of some-thing of immense realness, but of which you lack all true

perceptual knowledge. Like Lat. 85° N.—men had returned
and guaranteed you a pretty rum existence. The drifting un-
wholesomeness of incinerator smoke hurt his eyes, in which
superficial discomfort the conjectured miseries of the next
day and tomorrow lost themselves.

Reveille at 4.30 with its sleepy stretching and heavy
irksome return of consciousness—the letting in of the beginnings of morning, an icy filtering through, with the
drawing back of bolts; creeping into frowsy dank recesses,
a gusty-cool, wisping the littered surface of body-steaming
hay. The gulped-down tea, the distribution of eked-out
bacon, the wiping dry of mess-tins with straw—they must
carry this day's bread. The score of last-minute scamper-
ings and searchings for things mislaid and the sudden heart
thump at small things of importance remembered too late
—no use now—leave the bloody thing.

The last few moments came, and became the past. The
last candle was snuffed out and thrust still warm at the
wick and pliable into your tunic pocket. Greatly encumbered bodies, swung with caution down, from ramshackle
lofts and upper places, and blundered out from small
openings below—a weighted colliding on the stones—
heel-irons, and butt-heel-irons clattering hollow[2]—confused voices resonant in the walled darkness. The hinged
gate noisily swung-to with the last departing. Only some
animal's hoof against her wooden stall made a muted knock-
ing, breaking from time to time upon the kindly creature's
breathing.

It was 5.55 when No. 7 and No. 8 formed two-deep in
platoon in the narrow lane that was the one exit from this
place to the broad paved grey way going east, and very
straight, with its flanking guard of trees.

Lieutenant Jenkins found them standing: standing easy,

standing heavily, with feet pressed down into the watery
deep ruts left by the wheels of farm-wains; tiny hay-stalks
clung to their equipment and in the soft clean fur of their
jerkins, which, yesterday brought from Ordnance, lent
them an unexpected contour and texture, and a rightness
—born of necessity.[3]

This button-sticked Pomeranian fudge and Corporal
Swivler's extree spit for his jim-crack numerals can't com-
pete—

La! they've lopped his scarlet facings for him.

On the wide pavé road they took their position behind
'A', moved left in fours, facing a futile chill sun; strong
wind shivered their left sides, and blued the bent knuckles
about the cold iron of their sloped rifles clasped. So that
they anticipated the order which would permit them to
march more freely, with irritable mutterings.

Half a kilometre this side of Z 19 d 2 3 they briefly
halted, came again to the slope—redressed and again moved
on. A General Officer, with two of his staff, sat on horses in
a triangular green where was a stone shrine in 1870 Gothic.
He took the salute as his four battalions passed. He spoke
once or twice briefly to his underlings; one of them made
notes on paper.

Number seven—eyes right.
Eyes front.
March at ease.
He acted the parade soldier well enough.
March easy.

Childs-bane!—old wall-eye sees your dirty billikin through
your navel.
She 'll nark Gertie's grubby shift.
He smells your private ditty-bag[4] from afar.

17

Amanuensis Nancy can't jot his damaging hogs-wash fast
    enough.
Cotsplut! there's bastards for you.
They'll feel the pinch alright at
Daffy Shenkin's Great Assize.
Roll on the Resurrection.
Send it down David.
Rend the middle air.
Send it down boy.[5]

 Each platoon in turn passed self-consciously beyond the
orbit of scrutiny; the Brigade Commander's penetrating,
fussily efficient eye, the insolent, indifferent glancing, of
his two young men.
 By a building of red brick, fronted with a yard, busy with
carts and blue-trousered men moving casks—the sound of
an hydraulic mechanism within—a traffic-control officer
watched the last files of the rear company lurch up with
all their gear; pack the outside seats.
 He waited until the last grey 'bus moved eastward with
its load, and went back to breakfast.

They heavily clambered down, in their nostrils an awareness and at all their sense-centres a perceiving of strange
new things.
 The full day was clear after the early rain. The great flats,
under the vacant sky, spread very far. It was not that the
look of the place was unfamiliar to you. It was at one to all
appearances with what you knew already. The sodden
hedgeless fields—the dykes so full to overflowing to bound
these furrows from these, ran narrow glassy demarkations.
The firm, straight-thrust, plumb-forward way, to march
upon; the black bundles labouring, bent to the turnips
for each wide plot; the same astonishing expanse of sky.

Truly the unseen wind had little but your nice body for its teeth—and 'o2 Weavel's snuffle would depress anyone —but what was the matter with that quite ordinary tree. That 's a very usual looking farm house. The road was as Napoleon had left it. The day itself was what you'd expect of December.

He noticed that the other three, his marching companions, in that section of four, were unusually silent, who normally were so boringly communicative. He supposed them too tired to talk. Certainly they might well be—the day had been strenuous enough from its sleepy beginnings at four o'clock—or did they share with him his inward restiveness, deep in the bowels, so dry for your tongue's root.

For half an hour they pushed on; an occasional voice— an N.C.O. checking some minor fault, someone asking a simple question of his fellow, someone's personal sense of irksomeness becoming audible in grumbled oaths. But for the most part it was a silent half hour, except for the regular beat of the feet on the stone sets; the outside men of each four slithering now and again on the too acute camber.

John Ball regained a certain quietness and an indifference to what might be, as his loaded body moved forward unchoosingly as part of a mechanism another mile or so.

They passed a small building lying back from the road, that appeared deserted, its roof and nearer wall damaged at some time and now repaired with boarding. Perhaps they'd had some kind of fire, at all events it looked sordid and unloved. He drew back into his but lately lifted gloom.

There was a temporary halt where a light railway met the road. Trucks filled with very new clean deal planking, stakes of pine, stacked neatly up, wooden frames, bales of wire-netting and other wire, hedge-hog like, in balls; a rigid medley thrown about—iron and wood and iron, made evidently to some precise requirement, shaped to some usage yet unknown to any of that halting company; who looked on wonderingly, with half inquisitive, half fearful, glancing. Anyway they wouldn't have railways very near the line—would they. They went on again more feebly, more pain in the soles of the feet—that renewal, and increase of aching, which comes after the brief halting. The sky maintained its clear serenity, no cloud at all sailed on its vastness at noon. John Ball stretched his neck to ease the pain of his valise-straps chafing, his eyes looked involuntarily, with his head's tilting. There spread before him on the blue warp above as though by a dexterous, rapid shuttling, unseen, from the nether-side, a patterning of intense white; each separate bright breaking through, sudden and with deliberate placing—a slow spreading out, a loss of compact form, drifting into an indeterminate mottling. He marvelled at these foreign clouds. There seemed in the whole air above but from no sensible direction, or point, a strong droning, as if a million bees were hiving to the stars.

They gazed upwards as they went, their ill-guided feet stumbling stupidly over filled-in circular roughnesses pitting the newly-mended road. Ten minutes passed uneventfully and in silence.

Close in left—large hole to right of road.

As each congested file skirted that cavity, apprehensive eyes glanced sideways, turned in unison, as though at a saluting base.

Eyes front can't you—open out again in those fours.

That hole was wide and very deeply conical—the hard cut stones split and dislodged lay all about for many yards, they had to step over the fragments as they passed. A message reached Mr. Jenkins, who halted them—the platoon in front moved on—leaving them standing. When they started again the platoon behind did not move with them.

One running back from No. 6 saluted.

Open out in two ranks sir—road block in centre sir.

Men were busy here shovelling rubble into a great torn
upheaval in the paving. A splintered tree scattered its
winter limbs, spilled its life low on the ground. They
stepped over its branches and went on. A cyclist slid in
haste from his machine, saluted, handed a written message
to the Company Commander, received back an initialled
slip, again saluted—sped on wheels away.

Must increase the pace a bit sergeant. Be careful not to
close on the people in front—we march by sections after
we pass—X 18 b 5—four, yes, after we pass the large
house—there—by the bend. You see it—no—yes, that one.

Moving by section of platoon their way inclined more
south and right, well shielded by trees. They became comforted in their mood and talked to each other and smoked.
They asked of each other why there seemed in that place
the sickly smell of pineapple. John Ball was puzzled, why
in his mouth and throat there seemed to be the astringency
of Parrish's Food—Aunt Woodman in Norwood kept it
in bottles.

A sharp inclination right, along a watery byway, open to
all the world, winding the recession of mangolds. A man
with his puttees fastened at the ankle, without tunic, his
cap at a tilt, emerged upon the landscape and took water
in a flexible green canvas bucket from the ditch, where a
newly painted board, bearing a map reference, marked the
direction of a gun-position. Tall uprights at regular intervals, to the north-east side of this path were hung with a
sagging netting—in its meshes painted bits of rag, bleached
with rain and very torn, having all the desolation peculiar
to things that functioned in the immediate past but which
are now no longer serviceable, either by neglect or by
some movement of events.

At a forking of the path were buildings, farm buildings,

like any others. The leading platoon carried on, took the way left.

No. 7 closed its sections and waited.

You bunch together before a tarred door. Chalk scrawls on its planking—initials, numbers, monograms, signs, hasty, half-erased, of many regiments. Scratched out dates measuring the distance back to antique beginnings.

Dragoons—one troop.

4th Hussars—'D' Squadron No. 3 Troop.

Numerals crossed slanting indecipherable allocations earlier still.

More clear, and very newly chalked, you read the title of your entering, and feel confident, as one who reads his own name in a church pew. '2 platoons, B Company', in large, ill-formed calligraphy, countermanding the shadowy ciphering of the previous occupants. Lance-Corporal Lewis pushed open the door—and you file in.

The straw was grey and used and not so plentiful as the heaped-up hay of their morning's rising.

All right in here—comfortable—let them get some rest— we parade at 5 o'clock.

Reveille ?—no—five this evening.

Scattered recumbent round the walls within, they listened with eagerness, the truth stole upon them. That night would be spent in some other place.

The more contriving had already sought out nails and hooks on which to hang their gear for the night, and to arrange, as best they might, their allotted flooring.

They would make order, for however brief a time, and in whatever wilderness.

Anyway, get what rest you can. I'll be along at 4.30— yes, everything, I'm afraid. There was talk of dumping valises⁶—yes—we're taking them in. I think greatcoats

22

folded—they may change that—waterproof capes worn.

Very good sir.

Oh, I forgot, there will be a rifle-inspection in an hour's time—yes, at 3.45.

I see sir, I'll get 'em on their rifles at once. Sergeant Snell's salute had not to it the usual perfection.

Some sleep if you can sergeant.

He walked slowly across the yard, meeting John Ball at the gate, carrying a mess-tin of water.

Have you a match Ball.

Confusedly he put his mess-tin down, to search his pockets. Mr. Jenkins tapped the end of a cigarette on the broken gate-post, his head turned away and toward the lane, toward the shielded batteries, toward the sagging camouflage. The jaunty bombardier had come again for water—his tunic on, the day was getting colder. His chill fingers clumsy at full trouser pocket, scattered on the stones: one flattened candle-end, two centime pieces, pallid silver sixpence, a length of pink Orderly Room tape, a latch-key. The two young men together glanced where it lay incongruous, bright between the sets. Keys of Stondon Park. His father has its twin in his office in Knightryder Street. Keys of Stondon Park in French farmyard. Stupid Ball, it's no use here, so far from its complying lock. Locks for shining doors for plaster porches, gentlemen of the 6.18, each with a shining key, like this strayed one in the wilderness. They yawn into their news sheets—the *communiqué* is much as yesterday.

Will you have these sir.

Thanks—go in and get some sleep.

The sergeant's head thrust out from the barn door opening.

Mr. Jenkins's shoulders hunched—he blames Mr. May.

Keep them—wont you?

Thanks.

On addressing commissioned officers — it was his favourite theme. John Ball stood patiently, waiting for the eloquence to spend itself. The tedious flow continued, then broke off very suddenly. He looked straight at Sergeant Snell enquiringly—whose eyes changed queerly, who ducked in under the low entry. John Ball would have followed, but stood fixed and alone in the little yard—his senses highly alert, his body incapable of movement or response. The exact disposition of small things—the precise shapes of trees, the tilt of a bucket, the movement of a straw, the disappearing right boot of Sergeant Snell—all minute noises, separate and distinct, in a stillness charged through with some approaching violence—registered not by the ear nor any single faculty—an on-rushing pervasion, saturating all existence; with exactitude, logarithmic, dial-timed, millesimal—of calculated velocity, some mean chemist's contrivance, a stinking physicist's destroying toy.

He stood alone on the stones, his mess-tin spilled at his feet. Out of the vortex, rifling the air it came—bright, brass-shod, Pandoran; with all-filling screaming the howling crescendo's up-piling snapt. The universal world, breath held, one half second, a bludgeoned stillness. Then the pent violence released a consummation of all burstings out; all sudden up-rendings and rivings-through—all taking-out of vents—all barrier-breaking—all unmaking. Pernitric begetting—the dissolving and splitting of solid things. In which unearthing aftermath, John Ball picked up his mess-tin and hurried within; ashen, huddled, waited in the dismal straw. Behind 'E' Battery, fifty yards down the road, a great many mangolds, uprooted, pulped, congealed with chemical earth, spattered and made slippery the rigid boards leading to the emplacement. The sap of vegetables slobbered the spotless breech-block of No. 3 gun.

PART 3

STARLIGHT ORDER

Men went to Catraeth, familiar with laughter.
The old, the young, the strong, the weak.

Proceed . . . without lights . . . prostrate before it . . . he
begins without title, silently, immediately . . . in a low voice,
omitting all that is usually said. No blessing is asked, neither
is the kiss of peace given . . . he sings alone.[2]

Cloud shielded her bright disc-rising yet her veiled influence illumined the texture of that place, her glistening on
the saturated fields; bat-night-gloom intersilvered where she
shone on the mist drift,
when they paraded
    at the ending of the day, unrested
                        bodies, wearied from the morning,
    troubled in their minds,
                    frail bodies loaded over much,
'prentices bearing this night the full panoply, the complex
paraphernalia of their trade.
    The ritual of their parading was fashioned to austerity, and
bore a new directness.
They dressed to an hasty alignment,
they did not come to the slope;
by a habit of their bodies, conforming to monosyllabic, low-
voiced, ordering.
    They moved rather as grave workmen than as soldiers from
their billets' brief shelter.

For John Ball there was in this night's parading, for all the
fear in it, a kind of blessedness, here was borne away with
yesterday's remoteness, an accumulated tedium, all they'd
piled on since enlistment day: a whole unlovely order this
night would transubstantiate, lend some grace to. Knobbed
nickel at under arm thumb at seam smart cut away from the
small[3] (and hair on upper lip invests him with little charm)
re-numbering re-dressing two-inch overlap pernickety posh-
ers-up, drum-majors knashing in their Blancoed paradises,

27

twisted pipe-clayed knots for square-pushing shoulders,⁴ tin
soldiers, toy soldiers, militarymen in rows—you somehow
suffer the pain of loss—it's an ungracious way of life—but-
tocked lance-jacks crawling for the second chevron—Band-
boys in The Wet⁵—the unnamable nostalgia of depots.

He would hasten to his coal-black love: he would breathe
more free for her grimly embrace, and the reality of her. He
was glad when they said to him—and the free form of it:
    When you're ready No. 7—sling those rifles—move them
on sergeant, remain two-deep on the road—we join 5, 6 and
8 at the corner—don't close up—keep your distance from
No. 6—be careful not to close up—take heed those leading
files—not to close on No. 6—you're quite ready?—very
good.
    Move on . . . move 'em on.
    Get on . . . we're not too early.
    Informal directness buttressed the static forms—ritual
words made newly real.
    The immediate, the nowness, the pressure of sudden, modi-
fying circumstance—and retribution following swift on
disregard; some certain, malignant opposing, brought in-
telligibility and effectiveness to the used formulae of command; the liturgy of their going-up assumed a primitive
creativeness, an apostolic actuality, a correspondence with
the object, a flexibility.
    Back past the white board at the juncture of the ditches,
the gossamer swaying camouflage to drape the night-lit
sky. The bombardier was whistling at his work on No. 3.
Night-lines⁶ twinkle above the glistening vegetable damp:
men standing illusive in the dark light about some systemed
task, transilient, regularly spaced, at kept intervals, their
feet firm stanced apart, their upper bodies to and fro . . . slid
through live, kindly, fingers

cylindrical shining
death canistering
the dark convenient dump, momentarily piling.

Horses draw out to the road, lightly, unballast—tail-board
pins play free and road-sets flint for the striking, at slither
and recover.

One leaping up behind who cries out—tosses some bulging sack:
For the wagon lines[7]—forgot last night—
good night Dai.
Good night Mick.
Good night Master
may Barbara
bless the bed that you go to
and keep
her partial suffrages against his evening hate.[8]
Good night Parrott
good night Bess.
Good night good night—buck up—he gets nasty later on.
Good night, bon swores 'Waladr. Nos dawch, Jac-y-dandi.[9]
Night night.

They halted for the hurrying team; envying the drivers their
waiting beds.

No. 6 moved, just visible, in front.

Guides met them at an appointed place; pilots who knew
the charting of this gaining wilderness; the road continued
its undeviating eastward thrust, its texture more tedious to
the feet with each going forward; the road-pittings, irregularly filled, becoming now the greater surface. They passed
a place where was a ruin, they heard muted voices: the dark
seemed gaining on the hidden moon—No. 6, in front, no
longer seen.

A fanned-flashing to the higher dislocations—how piteous the torn small twigs in the charged exposure: an instant, more intenser, dark.

Throbbing on taut ear-drum
boomed hollow out-rushing and the
shockt recoil
the unleashing
a releasing.

Far thuddings faintly heard in the stranger-world: where the road leads, where no man goes, where the straight road leads; where the road had led old men asleep on wagons beneath the green, girls with baskets, linen-palled, children dawdling from the Mysteries on a Sunday morning.

Field-battery flashing showed the nature of the place the kindlier night had hid: the tufted avenue denuded, lopt, deprived of height; stripped stumps for flowering limbs—this discontent makes winter's rasure creaturely and kind.

A sand-bagged barrier checks the road by half.

They were told to halt.

Rain began to fall.

A shielded lantern hung by the barrier, cast refracted ray like gusty rush-light gleam for under facets, on his Webley's lanyard-ring; on the rimless pince-nez of the other.

He was talking to the commander of No. 6; a huddled sentry, next them, by the wall of bags. The rain increased where they miserably waited, there was no sound at all but of its tiresome spatter; the clouded moon quite lost her influence, the sodden night, coal-faced. They lighted saturated cigarettes.

Wind gusts rose to swirl and frisk half-severed, swung branches; jammed wood split to twisted screechings. Away somewhere, gun with lifted muzzle, Jaguar-coughs, across the rain. While they wait in the weather by the barrier, and half doze over their rifle-stocks.

Someone seemed to be stirring in front; they bunch their heads in the next file: Pass the message back—who—where's the sergeant—to move on.

Stand fast you.

Stand fast 2, 3 and 4.

Move on No. 1—get 'em into file corporal—move on by section—put those cigarettes out—no lights past the barrier. Past the little gate.

Mr. Jenkins watched them file through, himself following, like western-hill shepherd.

Past the little gate,

into the field of upturned defences,

into the burial-yard—

the grinning and the gnashing and the sore dreading—nor saw he any light in that place.[10]

Wind's high-rising, rustling inter-lined Burberry, damp-flapping across knee-joint.

Jaguar-gun, wind carried, barks again from X zone.

In virid-bright illumining he sees his precious charge, singly going, each following each, fleecy coated, and they themselves playing the actor to their jackets on sheepwalk's lateral restricting, between the lopped colonnade.

Shuts down again the close dark; the stumbling dark of the blind, that Breughel knew about—ditch circumscribed; this all depriving darkness split now by crazy flashing; marking hugely clear the spilled bowels of trees, splinter-spike, leper-ashen, sprawling the receding, unknowable, wall of night—the slithery causeway—his little flock, his armed bishopric, going with weary limbs.

'44 Adams was the rear man in that filed-flock; who stopped suddenly, ill controlled and stumblingly, whose hinder-gear collided, in the fickle flashing with the near-stepping, of many thoughts care-full, head down bent platoon commander.

Sorry sir they've—Get on man get on, you'll lose connection.

Sorry sir they've stopped in front.

Pass up message from officer in rear—Message from in front sir — they've halted sir — to right of road sir — road blocked, sir.

So they stood waiting; thick-textured night cloaked.

So he dreamed where he slept where he leaned, on piled material in the road's right ditch.

Stepping over things in the way, can't lift knee high enough —it makes the thigh ache so—more of them in front as far as you can see—can't go to left or right—this restricting corridor—higher ones, hurdles on 'jerks-ground':
Up, up—o-ver
Up pup—o-verr.

Gorilla-sergeant, in striped singlet, spring-toed, claps his hands like black-man-master: Get over — you Ball — you cowson.

Obstacles on jerks-course made of wooden planking—his night phantasm mazes a pre-war, more idiosyncratic skein, weaves with stored-up very other tangled threads; a wooden donkey for a wooden hurdle is easy for a deep-sleep transformation-fay to wand
carry you on dream stuff
up the hill and down again
show you sights your mother knew,
show you Jesus Christ lapped in hay with Uncle Eb and his diamond dress-stud next the ox and Sergeant Milford taking his number, juxtapose, dovetail, web up, any number of concepts, and bovine lunar tricks.

Hurdles on jerks-course all hard-edged for inefficient will not obtain the prize ones, who beat the air; wooden donkeys for the shins of nervous newcomer to the crowded night-class, step over to get your place beside Mirita; it's a winding mile between hostile matter from the swing-door, in and out the easel forest in and out barging, all of 'em annoyed with the past-pushing with clumsy furniture. Stepping over Miss Weston's thrown about belongings. Across his night dream the nightmare awaking:

Move on—get a move on—step over—up over.

And sleepy eyed see Jimmy Grove's[11] irregular bundle-figure, totter upward labouringly, immediately next in front, his dark silhouette sways a moment above you—he drops away into the night and your feet follow where he seemed to be. Each in turn labours over whatever it is—this piled broken-ness—dragged over and a scared hurrying on—the slobber was ankle-deep where you found the road again.

Mr. Jenkins read his watch while he waited for the last man; they'd been going just an hour; he followed on again after old Adams of Section 4. Intermittent gun flashing had ceased; nothing at all was visible; it still rained in a settled fashion, acutely aslant, drenching the body; they passed other bodies, flapping, clinking, sodden; moving west, moving in-visible, never known, no word said, no salutation. A straggler following—fleet-passing sound-wraith, coughing hollowly in his running to catch up; coughing like strangers do at night in some other room, in a stranger-house; and some other follows him, hurrying faster by—still coughing far down the road, heard in wind lull—ought to do something about it; see the M.O. or something, it's ridiculous not to do something about it ... out on a night like this. A cold place—O, there couldn't be a colder place for my love to wander in—and it's only early on, you wait till March and the lengthening light on the low low lands.[12]

Mind the hole sir—mind the hole, keep left—go slower in front—they've halted sir.

He pushed forward to investigate.

Is that you sir, Sergeant Snell sir, we've lost connection with No. 6, sir—they must have turned off·sir—back there sir.

Where's the guide.

With No. 6 sir.

Lovely for them—we'd better keep the road, get to the rear, see no one falls out, see them all up—move on No. 7, don't lose connection—wait for the man behind —move on.

There's no kind light to lead: you go like a motherless child —goddam guide's done the dirty, and is our Piers Dorian Isambard Jenkins—adequately informed—and how should his inexperience not be a broken reed for us—and fetch up in Jerry's bosom.

Slower in front—slower,
not so regardless of this perturbation in the rear; for each false footfall piles up its handicap proportionately backward, and No. 1's mole hill is mountainous for No. 4; and do we trapse dementedly round phantom mulberry bush . . . can the young bastard know his bearings.

Keep well to left—take care with these messages.

About their feet the invisible road surface split away in a great, exactly drawn circle; they felt its vacuous pitness in their legs, and held more closely to the banked-up solid.

The rain stopped.
She drives swift and immaculate out over, free of these obscuring waters; frets their fringes splendid.
A silver hurrying to silver this waste
silver for bolt-shoulders
silver for butt-heel-irons
silver beams search the interstices, play for breech-blocks

underneath the counterfeiting bower-sway; make-believe a
silver scar with drenched tree-wound ; silver-trace a festooned slack; faery-bright a filigree with gooseberries and
picket-irons[13]—grace this mauled earth—
transfigure our infirmity—
shine on us.
I want you to play with
and the stars as well.[14]
 Received,
curtained where her cloud captors
pursue her bright
pursue her darkly
detain her—
when men mourn for her, who go stumbling, these details
for the ambuscade praise her, for an adjutrix; like caved robbers on a Mawddwy hill—the land waste as far as English
Maelor; green girls in broken keeps have only mastiff-guards
—like the mademoiselle at Croix Barbée.[15]

Transferred Warwick subaltern with his Welsh platoon
passed them in the moon, his thoughts on green places where
the counties meet; they're still secure at Bourton-on-the-
Water. She did her knitting to this comforter staying with
Aunt Mildred in Stretton—they left Tite Street to avoid
the raids.
The precious: she's made it of double warp.
The cowsons: they've banned 'em[16]—they do deaden the
sound a bit—but not much use hearing It coming.
 The Mercian dreamer and his silent men all pass in turn,
followed on by more, who, less introspect, wish a brief good
night.
 It's cushy[17] mate, it's cushy—
it's cushy up there but
buck up past Curzon Post—he has it taped.

Good night chum.
Good night.

The repeated passing back of aidful messages assumes a cadency.
Mind the hole
mind the hole
mind the hole to left
hole right
step over
keep left, left.

One grovelling, precipitated, with his gear tangled, struggles to feet again:
Left be buggered.

Sorry mate — you all right china? — lift us yer rifle — an' don't take on so Honey—but rather, mind
the wire here[18]
mind the wire
mind the wire
mind the wire.

Extricate with some care that taut strand—it may well be you'll sweat on its unbrokenness.

Modulated interlude, violently discorded—mighty, fanned-up glare, to breach it: light orange flame-tongues in the long jagged water-mirrors where their feet go, the feet that come shod, relief bringing—bringing release to these from Wigmore and Woofferton. Weary feet: feet bright, and gospelled, for these, of Elfael and Ceri.

We're relieving the Borderers—two platoons of their 12th thet was—in wiv the Coldstreams[19]—relieved be our 14th.

Sergeant Snell was informed as to the disposition of units.

The colonnade to left and right kept only shorn-off column shafts, whose branchy capitals strew the broken sets. Where

roofless walls, reinforced with earth-filled sacks fronted the
road, on a board, moon lighted, they read as they filed past:

TO
MOGGS HOLE
NO LOITERING BY DAY

and from its peg, a shell-case swung,[20] free of the sand-
bagged wall.

Sometimes his bobbing shape showed clearly; stiff mario-
nette jerking on the uneven path; at rare intervals he saw the
whole platoon, with Mr. Jenkins leading.

Wired dolls sideway inclining, up and down nodding, fantastic troll-steppers in and out the uncertain cool radiance,
amazed crook-back miming, where sudden chemical flare,
low-flashed between the crazy flats, flood-lit their sack-
bodies, hung with rigid properties—
the drop falls,
you can only hear their stumbling off, across the dark pro-
scenium.

So they would go a long while in solid dark, nor moon, nor
battery, dispelled.

Feet plodding in each other's unseen tread. They said no
word but to direct their immediate next coming, so close
behind to blunder, toe by heel tripping, file-mates; blind on-
following, moving with a singular identity.

Half-minds, far away, divergent, own-thought thinking,
tucked away unknown thoughts; feet following file friends,
each his own thought-maze alone treading; intricate, twist
about, own thoughts, all unknown thoughts, to the next so
close following on.

He hitched his slipping rifle-sling for the hundredth time

over a little where the stretched out surface skin raw rubbed away at his clavicle bone. He thought he might go another half mile perhaps—it must be midnight now of some day of the week. He turned his tired head where the sacking-shield swayed.

Where a white shining waned between its hanging rents, another rises and another; high, unhurrying higher, clear, pale, light-ribbons; very still-bright and bright-showered descent.

Spangled tapestry swayed between the uprights; camouflage-net, meshed with plunging star-draught.

Bobbing night-walkers go against the tossing night-flares.

Intermittent dancing lights betray each salient twist and turn; tiny flickers very low to the south—their meandering world-edge prickt out bright.

Rotary steel hail spit and lashed in sharp spasms along the vibrating line; great solemn guns leisurely manipulated their expensive discharges at rare intervals, bringing weight and full recession to the rising orchestration.

As suddenly the whole world would slip back into a mollifying, untormented dark; their aching bodies knew its calm.

What moved in front is rigid with a clumsy suddenness:
Message back—they've halted mate.
What's that.
We've got to halt, pass it back.
He just muttered halt without a turn of the head.
Get on get on—we'll lose connection.
They've halted I tell you, pass it back.
Dark chain of whisperings link by link jerked each one motionless.
A mile you say?
About a mile sir—straight on sir—machine gun, sir, but they're spent, most of 'em—but further on sir, by Foresters

Lane—he's got a fixed-rifle on the road[21]—two of our people
—last night sir.

The Borderer sergeant bid good night and passed like his
predecessors toward the west.

'Night sergeant.

'Night chaps—yes cushy—but buck up on the road.

The hide and seek of dark-lit light-dark yet accompanied
their going; the journeying moon yet curtained where she
went.

Once when her capricious shining, when she briefly aided
them, John Ball raised up his head:
In the cleft of the rock they served Her in anticipation—and
over the hill-country that per-bright Shiner stood for Her
rod-budding (he kept his eyes toward the swift modulations
of the sky, heaven itinerant hurrying with his thought hast-
ing)—but that was a bugger of a time ago.[22]

Nuvver 'ole mate—pass it back—largish an' all—look where
yer going.

He took notice of his stepping, his eyes left their star-
gazing.

Slime-glisten on the churnings up, fractured earth pilings,
heaped on, heaped up waste; overturned far throwings; tottering perpendiculars lean and sway; more leper-trees pitted, rownsepykèd out of nature, cut off in their sap-rising.

Saturate, littered, rusted coilings, metallic rustlings, thin
ribbon-metal chafing—rasp low for some tension freed; by rat,
or wind, disturbed. Smooth-rippled discs gleamed, where
gaping craters, their brimming waters, made mirror for the
sky procession—bear up before the moon incongruous souvenirs. Margarine tins sail derelict, where little eddies quivered,
wind caught, their sharp-jagged twisted lids wrenched back.

From chance hardnesses scintilla'd strikings, queer reboundings at spiteful tangent sing between your head and his.

That one went up at an unexpected nearness. The faraway
dancing barrier surprisingly much nearer; you even hear the
dull report quickly upon the uprising light; and now, right
where they walked, at sudden riot against your unsuspecting
ear-drums, a Vicker's team discovers its position, by low
builded walls of sacks; and men worked with muffled ham-
merings of wood on wood; and the front files pause again.

Yes—who are you—get your men into cover while they're
halted. He flashed his torch on the other's uniform; which
near brightness made them hug in closer, their apprentice-
wisdom shocked.

A bleeding brass hat.

The bastard'll have us all blown up—softly, and consider
his plenary powers, it's that cissy from Brigade, the one wat
powders.

You've lost your guide—you can read the map, anyway,
it's a plumb straight road—you've three hundred yards to
the communication trench—turn left into Sandbag Alley—
right at the O.B.L.[23]—left into Oxford Street—get along
quickly—he has us enfiladed.

Thank you sir, good night sir.

He lights another cigarette. His match is like a beacon in
this careful dark. His runner emerges from the bags on the
left.

Yes sir—to the car sir?

No, leave me at Lansdowne Post—tell him to bring it up
Foresters—Oh yes he can, perfectly well—tell him mess is
at 8.0 not 8.30.

And the servants of the rich are off on the word: Bo!—
what I mean to say is you don't want to lose the job
nor 'get returned'

to march with these
gay companions—
He's near enough already—he passes most horribly close—
and these go out to jig with him on slanting floors.

No. 7 to move on—not far now little children—try to keep
the pace.

The road, broken though it was, seemed a firm causeway
cutting determinedly the insecurity that lapped its path,
sometimes the flanking chaos overflowed its madeness, and
they floundered in unstable deeps; chill oozing slime high
over ankle; then they would find it hard and firm under their
feet again, the mason work in good order, by some freak, intact. Three men, sack-buskined to the hips, rose like judgment wraiths out of the ground, where brickwork still stood
and strewn red dust of recent scattering dry-powdered the
fluid earth; and your nostrils draw on strangely pungent air.

No sir—further on sir, but you'd better go by the trench,
he's on this bit—yes to Pioneer Keep, then into the front line
—it's right of this road—the O.B.L. sir?—we stopt using it
a week back sir, he knocked it flat when they went over from
The Neb—you can chance the road sir, but he's on it—all the
time—three of the Coldstreams, only yesterday—he's traversing now—better get in, sir.

He filed the leading section behind low harbouring earth;
2, 3 and 4 following; and last came Sergeant Snell, his mess-
tin like a cullender.

And he quietened down—nothing but a Lewis gun, far
away.

I think we'll use the road—move out No. 4—move out
the next section—move on—get those men out, sergeant
—move on—No. 4 leading.

They stepped delicately from this refuge.

They've halted in front sir.

German gunner, to and fro, leisurely traversed on his night-target.

Sergeant Snell with No. 4 crumpled, low crouched, in in-effectual ditch-shelter.

All right in front—you all right Sergeant Snell?—move your men on, sergeant.

Pass up the message—move on in front—move on imme-diately.

Pass it up—what's the game.

There's a windy tripehound.

Step on it for christ's sake, you're holding up Duration.

And this burst spent, they moved on again, alertness bring-ing new strength to their ill condition; awareness for their aching limbs: their great frailty was sufficient body for the forming of efficient act.

With his first traversing each newly scrutinised his neigh-bour; this voice of his Jubjub gains each David his Jonathan; his ordeal runs like acid to explore your fine feelings; his near presence at break against, at beat on, their convenient hier-archy.

Lance-Corporal Lewis sings where he walks, yet in a low voice, because of the Disciplines of the Wars.[24] He sings of the hills about Jerusalem, and of David of the White Stone.[25]

Now when a solitary star-shell rose, a day-brightness illu-mined them; long shadows of their bodies walking, darken-ing out across the fields; slowly contracting with the light's rising, grotesquely elongating with its falling — this large lengthening is one with all this other.

Machine-gunner in Gretchen Trench[26] remembered his night target. Occasionally a rifle bullet raw snapt like tenuous hide whip by spiteful ostler handled. On both sides the artillery was altogether dumb.

Appear more Lazarus figures, where water gleamed between dilapidated breastworks, blue slime coated, ladling with wooden ladles; rising, bending, at their trench dredging. They speak low. Cold gurgling followed their labours. They lift things, and a bundle-thing out; its shapelessness sags. From this muck-raking are singular stenches, long decay leavened; compounding this clay, with that more precious, patient of baptism; chemical-corrupted once-bodies. They've served him barbarously—poor Johnny—you wouldn't desire him, you wouldn't know him for any other. Not you who knew him by fire-light nor any of you cold-earth watchers, nor searchers under the flares.[27]

Each night freshly degraded like traitor-corpse, where his heavies flog and violate; each day unfathoms yesterday unkindness; dung-making Holy Ghost temples.

They bright-whiten all this sepulchre with powdered chloride of lime. It's a perfectly sanitary war.

R.E.s, sir—yes sir, Sandbag Alley—leads into the O.B.L. sir —water-logged all the way sir—well above the knee sir— best keep the road—turn off left at Edgware, right at Hun Street sir—straight to the front line sir, brings you out be 'P' Sap, you couldn't miss it sir, not if you wanted to—we've a bit of a dump at the turn sir—our sergeant's there, with a carrying party—only just gone up sir.

The sapper returned to his baling; they heard him and his mates low mumbling; they heard the freed passage of the water sluice away, with the dreadful lifting-out of obstacles.

Close up in file and halt, pass it back quietly—move on until the last man is in the trench, and stand fast—pass it up when you're all in—see to that, sergeant.

Mr. Jenkins found his speech low-toned and regulated, lest he should wake the slumbering secrets of that place. A pallid Very-light climbed up from away in front. This gate of Mars armipotente, the grisly place, like flat painted scene in top-lights' crude disclosing. Low sharp-stubbed tree-skeletons, stretched slow moving shadows; faintest mumbling heard just at ground level. With the across movement of that light's shining, showed long and strait the dark entry, where his minis-trants go, by tunnelled ways, whispering.[28]

Step down—
step down and keep a bit left—keep your rifles down—mind the wire
mind the wire—
be careful of the wire.

The long professed sergeant of engineers; '04, Time Ex-pired, out since the Marne; tempered to night watchings, whole armoured against this sorry place; considerate of sluices, revetting frames and corrugated iron; of sapping to his second line, of mines and countermines, who dreamed of pontoons in open places, of taking over from the cavalry; stood at the trench head, and kindly, in a quiet voice, guided their catechumen feet:

Seem pretty bitched—but they'll soon shape—get 'em in quickly corporal, it's not too healthy here.

Far gone before the mind could register the passage, shells of high velocity over their trench-entering: Four separate, emptying detonations.

He's on Mogg's again—he's using H.E.—hope to christ the relief's through—it's that blasted Euston Road tramway that attracts him.

Edgware Trench, like a river's lock-gates, marked a new mood for the highway, which bore on still straightly; but from this bar, to litter its receding eastward surface, were strewn, uncleared, untouched, the souvenirs of many days; by no one walked upon, except perhaps some more intrepid Runner or charmed-life Linesman, searching, prying, cat-eyed, high and low diligently nosing, like pearl of great price seeker, for his precious rubber coiling — or more rarely a young gentleman from Division made bold by other considerations. He raises hell if one is late for mess.

All in sir—last man up—pass it up to move on—to move along—to move on quietly.

You step down between inward inclining, heavily bulged, walls of earth; you feel the lateral slats firm foothold. Squeaking, bead-eyed hastening, many footed hurrying, accompanying each going forward.

Break in the boards—pass it back.

The fluid mud is icily discomforting that circles your thighs; and Corporal Quilter sprawls full length; two of them help him to his feet, his rifle like a river-bed salvaged antique—which dark fumbling assistance brings the whole file to a standstill—who call out huskily, to move on; to get a move on, and now perversely—slower in front, go slower in front.

John Ball cries out to nothing but unresponsive narrowing earth. His feet take him upward over high pilings—down again to the deep sludge. There is no one before him where the way loses its identity in a network of watery ditches; he chooses the middle ditch, seen in the light's last flicker. Beneath his feet, below the water, he feels again the wooden flooring, and round the next bend in another light's rising the jogging pack of Aneirin Lewis—and heard him singing, very low, as he went.

So they will continue: each step conditioned, every yard subtly other in direction from the last, their bodies' angle and inclination strictly determined by this winding corridor, by the floor's erratic levels. At some points new built walls rose above their heads, their feet going confidently on neat laid engineer work—but here again hastily thrown-up earth insufficiently filled wide breaches, and they went exposed from the waist upward.

Pass it along—stand to left of trench—make way for carrying party.

Gretchen Trench gunner resumes his traversing. They low-crouched on haunches where the duckboard slats float. The freshly-set sand-bags fray and farrow; the hessian jets loose earth—clammy sprinklings, cold for your vertebrae. You hug lower crumpled against the quivering hurdle-stake.[29]

Evidently that carrying-party had decided to halt. Gretchen-trench gunner lowered his sights to 'Y' target, making taller men stoop, hunchbackwise out in 'P' sap.

Peering up from their crouching, feel solid, shadowy, careful past-pushing, leg moving rigid, awkward, lengthway, negotiating.

The night was at its darkest, you couldn't see the nearest object.

Go easy chum—
keep low here—steady a bit, lift up a bit—all right your end? —you over—over—bit of a weight Joe.

They go like that, like bleedin' lead.

Metalled eyelet hole in waterproof pall hanging glides cold across your upward tilted cheek with that carrying party's unseen passing—the smell of iodine hangs about when it's used so freely.

You can hear the stumbling, dead-weighted, bearers, very tortuously make winding progress back; low-voiced questioned, here and there, by these waiting, latest ones.

Private Watcyn calls Lance-Corporal Lewis from round an earth wall's turn, who nudges Private Ball who drags forward saturated limbs; water pours from his left boot as he lifts it clear. Scrapings and dull joltings, heavy, ill-controlled lurching, disturbed water gurgles with each man's footfall; they move ten yards further.

Mind the wire, china[30]

        —keep yourself low.

Bodies move just at head level, outside the trench; hollow unreal voices, reaching the ear unexpectedly, from behind or round the traverse bend, like the shouting at the immediate door comes on you from a far window:

I've found it Bertie, I've got 'D' and 'C'.

Telephonic buzzing makes the wilderness seem curiously homely; the linesman's boot implicates someone's tackle passing.

Sorry son—sorry.

He continues his song; he beats time with his heels thudding the trench-wall, his trade in his lap:

    Kitty Kitty isn't it a pity
    in the City[31]—it's a bad break, Bertie.

They bend low over, intently whistling low, like a mechanic's mate. They secure it with rubber solution; they pick their way, negotiating unseen wire, they remember the lie of the land with accuracy; they kick tins gratuitously, they go with light hearts; they walk naked above the fosse, they despise a fenced place; they are warned for Company Office. They pull at his decanter while he sleeps; they elude quartermasters; they know the latest—whispered however so low.[32]

The night dilapidates over your head and scarlet lightning annihilates the nice adjustment of your vision, used now to, and cat-eyed for the shades. You stumble under this latest demonstration; white-hot nine-inch splinters hiss, water-tempered, or slice the cross-slats between his feet—you hurry in your panic, which hurrying gives you clumsy foot-hold, which falling angers you, and you are less afraid; you call them all bastards—you laugh aloud.

Shrapnel salvos lift to the front line; rapid burst on burst. After a while it would be quiet again. There was no retalia-tion—not this early on.

And where the earth-works forked, the clipt hierarchic word, across the muted half-sounds connatural to the place, in some fashion reformed them, brought to them some assur-ance and token of normality.

Pass Relief.

Major Cantelupe?—no sir—going his rounds sir—th' ad-jutant?—at mess, sir.

The drawn back sacking loosed a triangle of consoling candle light.

He comes again; they stir where they heap like sawn logs diversely let to lie; they assemble their bodies on the narrow footing; they move on without sensation. The water's level is higher with each turn of the trench; the detached boards, on being trod on, at the nearer end, rise perpendicular for your embarrassment. Another salvo for the line—Curzon Post—Mogg's Hole.

And now at another forked-way, voices, and heavy material in contact, as if a gardener made firm a sloping pleasance; and someone coughs restrainedly and someone sings freely:

> O dear what can the matter be
> O dear what can the matter be
> O dear what can the matter be
> Johnny's so long at the Fair.

And from these also, the file moves on; the sound of them, and his singing, like some unexpected benignity you come on at a street-bend.

Until dim flickerings light across; to fade where the revetment changes direction, and overhead wire catches oblique ray cast up, and you know the homing perfume of wood burned, at the termination of ways; and sense here near habitation, a folk-life here, a people, a culture already developed, already venerable and rooted.

Follow on quietly No. 7—file in quietly—not such a pandemonium to advertise our advent.

You turn sharp left; the space of darkness about you seems of different shape and character; earth walls elbow at you in a more complicated way. You stand fast against the parados.

And you too are assimilated, you too are of this people—there will be an indelible characterisation—you'll tip-toe when they name the place.

Stand fast against the parados and let these eager bundles drag away hastily; and one turns on his going-out: Good night china—there's some dryish wood under fire-step[33]—in cubby-hole—good night.

Cushy—cushy enough—cushy, good night.

Good night kind comrade.

And the whole place empties; the narrow space clears. You feel about in the emptied darkness of it. They lose little time to make off, to leave you in possession.

Any of No. 7 here—Corporal Quilter here—Lance-Corporal Lewis—is Mathews here?

All of No. 1, sergeant—No. 1 Section complete, sergeant.

He posts his first night-sentries, there are ambiguous instructions; you will be relieved in two hours, the pass word is Prickly Pear.

And he, John Ball, his feet stayed-up above disintegrating earth—his breast at ground level. How colder each second you get stuck here after the sweat of it, and icy tricklings at

49

every cavity and wherever your finger-tips stray, the slug surface. He buried each hand in his great-coat sleeves, habitwise; the sagged headers sloped the parapet for a stall.

His eyeballs burned for the straining, was any proper object for the retina in all that blind night-drift, and sergeant said to keep a sharp look-out—to report any hostile movement—and the
counter-sign is
Prickly Pear
Prickly Pear
not to forget
important not to forget; important to keep your eyes open.

The light they sent up from the third bay[34] down, sinks feebly snuffed out in the weather, a yard before our wire; but its pallid arc sufficiently defines the paved way, preserving its camber and its straight-going from us to him; enough to shine on, long enough to show heaped-on rust heap, dripping water, like rained-on iron briary.

Peg sprawled tentacles, with drunken stakes thrust up rigid from the pocked earth. And to his immediate front, below the shelving ramp, a circular calm water graced the deep of a Johnson hole;[35] corkscrew-picket-iron half submerged, as dark excalibur, by perverse incantation twisted. And there, where the wire was thinnest: bleached, swaying, the dyed garment—like flotsam shift tossed up, from somebody other's dereliction.

At intervals lights elegantly curved above his lines, but the sheet-rain made little of their radiance. He heard, his ears incredulous, the nostalgic puffing of a locomotive, far off, across forbidden fields; and once upon the wind, from over his left shoulder, the nearer clank of trucks, ration-laden by Mogg's Hole.

PART 3

And the rain slacks at the wind veer
and she half breaks her cloud cover.

He puts up a sufficient light dead over the Neb; and in its
moments hanging, star-still, shedding a singular filament of
peace, for these fantastic undulations.

He angled rigid; head and shoulders free; his body's inclination at the extreme thrust of the sap head; outward toward
them, like the calm breasts of her, silent above the cutwater,
foremost toward them
and outmost of us, and
brother-keeper, and ward-watcher;
his mess-mates sleeping like long-barrow sleepers, their
dark arms at reach.
Spell-sleepers, thrown about anyhow under the night.
And this one's bright brow turned against your boot leather,
tranquil as a fer sídhe sleeper, under fairy tumuli, fair as
Mac Óg sleeping.[36]

Who cocks an open eye when you stamp your numbed feet
on the fire-step slats,
who tells you to stow it,
to put a sock in it,
to let a man sleep o' nights
— and redistributes his cramped limbs, and draws closer-
over his woollen comforter.

You shift on the boards a little to beat your toes against the
revetment where this other one sits upright, wakeful and less
fastidious, at an angle of the bay; who speaks without turning
his head to you, his eyes set on the hollow night beyond the
parados, he nursing his rifle, the bayonet's flat to his cheek-
bone; his syntax of the high hills—and the sharp inflexion:

Starving night indeed — important to maintain the circulation—there's starving for you—important to keep the
circulation.

Yes corporal.

Can you see anything, sentry.

Nothing corporal.

'o1 Ball is it, no.

Yes corporal.

Keep a sharp outlook sentry—it is the most elementary disciplines—sights at 350.

Yes corporal.

300 p'r'aps.

Yes corporal.

Starving as brass monkeys — as the Arctic bear's arse — Diawl![37] — starved as Pen Nant Govid, on the confines of hell.

Unwise it is to disturb the sentinel.

Do dogs of Annwn glast[38] this starving air—do they ride the trajectory zone, between the tangled brake above the leaning walls.

This seventh gate is parked[39] tonight.

His lamps hang in this black cold and hang so still; with this still rain slow-moving vapours wreathe to refract their clear ray—like through glassy walls that slowly turn they rise and fracture—for this fog-smoke wraith they cast a dismal sheen.[40]

What does he brew in his cauldron,

over there.

What is it like.

Does he watch the dixie-rim.

Does he watch—

the Watcher.

Does he stir his Cup—he blesses no coward's stir over there.

Does he watch for the three score hundred sleeping, or bent to their night tasks under the wall. In the complex galleries his organisation in depth[41] holds many sleeping, well-watched-for sleepers under the night flares.[42]

Old Adams, Usk, sits stark, he already regrets his sixty-

two years. His rifle-butt is a third foot for him,[43] all three supports are wood for him, so chill this floor strikes up, so this
chill creeps to mock his bogus 'listing age.

Forty-five—christ—forty-five in Her Jubilee Year, before the mothers of these pups had dugs to nourish them.

He grips more tightly the cold band of his sling-swivel;
he'd known more sodden, darker ways, below the Old
Working. He shifts his failing flanks along the clammy slats,
he settles next his lance-jack, he joins that muted song; together they sing low of the little cauldron, together they com-
memorate *Joni bach*.[44]

You draw out warm finger-tips:

Your split knuckles fumbling, foul some keen, chill-edged,
jack-spike jutting.

You could weep like a child,
you employ the efficacious word,[45]
to ease frustration;
be rid of,
last back-breaking straws.

At 350—slid up the exact steel, the graduated rigid leaf
precisely angled to its bed.

You remember the word of the staff instructor whose Kinross teeth bared; his bonnet awry, his broad bellow to make
you spring to it; to pass you out with the sixty-three parts
properly differentiated.[46]

You very gradually increase the finger-pressure to-ward
and up-ward.

The hollow-places and the upright things give back their
mimicry, each waking other, shockt far out. Short before his
parapet, disturbed wire tangs oddly for the erratic ricochet.

You draw back the bolt, you feel 'the empty' hollow-lob,
light against your boot lacing, you hear the infinitesimal
disturbance of water in the trench drain.

And the deepened stillness as a calm, cast over us—a

potent influence over us and him—dead-calm for this Sar-
gasso dank, and for the creeping things.
    You can hear the silence of it:
you can hear the rat of no-man's-land
rut-out intricacies,
weasel-out his patient workings,
scrut, scrut, sscrut,
harrow-out earthly, trowel his cunning paw;
redeem the time of our uncharity, to sap his own amphibious paradise.
    You can hear his carrying-parties rustle our corruptions
through the night-weeds—contest the choicest morsels in his
tiny conduits, bead-eyed feast on us; by a rule of his nature,
at night-feast on the broken of us.
    Those broad-pinioned;
blue-burnished, or brinded-back;
whose proud eyes watched
                the broken emblems
droop and drag dust,
suffer with us this metamorphosis.
    These too have shed their fine feathers; these too have
slimed their dark-bright coats; these too have condescended
to dig in.
    The white-tailed eagle at the battle ebb,
                where the sea wars against the river[47]
the speckled kite of Maldon
and the crow
have naturally selected to be un-winged;
to go on the belly, to
sap   sap   sap
with festered spines, arched under the moon; furrit with
whiskered snouts the secret parts of us.
    When it's all quiet you can hear them:
scrut scrut scrut

when it's as quiet as this is.

It's so very still.

Your body fits the crevice of the bay in the most comfortable fashion imaginable.

It's cushy enough.

The relief elbows him on the fire-step: All quiet china?—bugger all to report?—kipping mate?—christ, mate—you'll 'ave 'em all over.

PART 4

KING PELLAM'S LAUNDE

Like an home-reared animal in a quiet nook, before
his day came . . . before entering into the prison of
earth . . . around the contest, active and defensive,
around the fort, around the steep-piled sods.

PART 4

So thus he sorrowed till it was day and heard the foules sing, then somewhat he was comforted.[2]

Stand-to.[3]
Stand-to-arms.

Stealthly, imperceptibly stript back, thinning
night wraps
unshrouding, unsheafing—
and insubstantial barriers dissolve.
This blind night-negative yields uncertain flux.
At your wrist the phosphorescent dial describes the equal seconds.

The flux yields up a measurable body; bleached forms emerge and stand.

Where their faces turned, grey wealed earth bared almost of last clung weeds of night-weft—
behind them the stars still shined.

Her fractured contours dun where soon his ray would show more clear her dereliction.

Already before him low atmospheres harbingered his bright influence.

The filtering irradiance spread, you could begin to know that thing from this; this nearer from that away over.

There at ten o'clock from that leaning picket-iron, where the horizon most invented its character to their eyes straining, a changing dark, variant-textured, shaped to their very watching a wooded gradient.

Skin off those comforters—to catch with their
cocked ears
the early bird,
and meagre chattering of
December's prime
shrill over from
Biez wood.

Biez wood fog pillowed, by low mist isled, a play of hide and seek arboreal for the white diaphane.

To their eyes seeming a wood moving,

a moving grove advisioned.

Stand-to.

Stand-to.

Stand-to-arms.

Out there,
get out there
get into that fire trench.

Pass it along to Stand-to.

To peel back those eider-ducks me slumberin' lovelies—Prince Charming presents his compliments. Who's this John Moores in his martial cloak — get off it, wontcher — come away counterfeiting death — cantcher — hear the bird o' dawnin'—roll up—it's tomorrow alright.

Sergeant Charming's through your thorny slumbers, who bends over sweet Robin's rose cheek.

Morning sergeant—kiss me sergeant.

Whose toe porrects the ritual instrument to
break the spell to
resurrect the traverses.

Fog refracted, losing articulation in the cloying damp, the word of command unmade in its passage, mischiefed of the opaque air, mutated, bereaved of content, become an incoherent uttering, a curious bent cry out of the smarting drift, lost altogether—yet making rise again the grey bundles where they lie.

Sodden night-bones vivify, wet bones live.

With unfathomed passion—this stark stir and waking—contort the comic mask of these tragic japers.

With a great complaining, bay by bay, the furrowed traverses whiten and agitate.

PART 4

In 'P' sap, in 'Q' post,
in the fire-trench,
in Moggs Hole and Cats Post.

An eastward alignment of troubled, ashen faces; delicate mechanisms of nerve and sinew, grapple afresh, deal for another day; ill-matched contesting, handicapped out of reason, spirits at the ebb bear up; strung taut—by what volition keyed—as best they may.

As grievous invalids watch the returning light pale-bright the ruckled counterpane, see their uneased bodies only newly clear; fearful to know afresh their ill condition; yet made glad for that rising, yet strain ears to the earliest note—should some prevenient bird make his kindly cry.

Chance modulations in the fluxing mist, retro-fold roll, banked up—shield again the waking arborage.

With the gaining spread grey proto-light,
Morning-star pallid,
with the freshing day,
billowed damp more thickly hung yet whitened marvellously.

Nothing was defined beyond where the ground steepened just in front, where the trip-wire⁴ graced its snare-barbs with tinselled moistnesses.

Cloying drift-damp cupped in every concave place.

It hurts you in the bloody eyes, it grips chill and harmfully and rasps the sensed membrane of the throat; it's raw cold, it makes you sneeze—christ how cold it is.

With each moment passing — the opaque creeping into every crevice creeping, whiter — thick whitened, through-white, argent wall nebulous, took on, gave back, wholly reflected—till transfigured bright in each drenched dew particle—and the last Night-Sentry fidgets expectantly.

Keep on that fire-step.
Keep a sharp look out.

61

Sights down—watch the wire.

Keep your eyes skinned—it's a likely morning.

Behind them, beyond the brumous piling the last stars paled and twinkled fitfully, then faded altogether; knowing the mastery and their visitation; this beautiful one, his cloud garments dyed, ruddy-flecked, fleecy stoled; the bright healer, climbing certainly the exact degrees to his meridian. Yet the brume holds, defiantly, and with winter confident, to shroud the low places.

Even now you couldn't see his line, but it was much lighter. The wire-tangle hanging, the rank grass-tangle drenched, tousled, and the broken-tin glint showed quite clearly. Left and right in the fire-bays you could see: soft service-caps wet-moulded to their heads moving—their drawn upward cloth flaps like home-spun angler-heads—moving in the morning reaches.

Very slowly the dissipating mist reveals saturate green-grey flats, and dark up-jutting things; and pollard boles by more than timely wood-craftsman's cunning pruning dockt, —these weeping willows shorn.

And the limber-wheel, whose fractured spokes search upward vainly for the rent-off mortised-rim.

Now his wire thickets were visible as dark surf, before a strand rising to bleached wall of bags in neat layers. The light of day is fully master now, and all along, and from beyond the glistering wall, at irregular intervals, thin blue smoke rises straight, like robber-fire,[5] to thin-out amber against the eastern bright.

Over Biez Copse, as nainsook, low vapours yet could draw out tenuous parallels.

Head inclined to head in the bay to the left.

They call from round the traverse wall.

Pass it along to Stand-down.

Stand-down and clean rifles.
Post day-sentries—pass it along.

They stood miserably.

They stretched encumbered limbs to take their rifles, list-
less, bemused, to slowly scrape away the thicker mire caked,
with deadness in their eyes and hands as each to each they
spoke—like damned-corpse-gossiping, of hopeless bleedin'
dawns—then laught to see themselves so straitened, tricked
out in mudded stiffening.

They beat against the padded walls to flow again the ebb-
ing blood. They kicked the oozing sacks above the water surface till their toe-joints ached.

A lean lance-jack, grey faced with his one night's vicarious
office, called over the revetment.

Get on those rifles at once—get on with it.
Orl right Corp—got any gauze.
Wot we want is gauze.
Wot we want is boiling water,[6]
                    boiling bleedin' water.
Got any boiling water?

Then was great to-do and business, then were butt-heel-
irons opened, and splintering of thumb nails with the
jammed metal, and jack-knife blades shivered.

Got any oil.
Why don't you go to Sergeant and get
for yourselves.
Why didn't you ask the Quarter-bloke
back there.

Only a drop, china, just for the bolt—just a spot—be a kind
virgin—he's coming round the bend—he's doing No. 5—just
a spot.

Then was a pulling through of barrels and searching of minute vents and under-facets with pins, and borrowing of small necessaries to do with this care of arms. Then began prudent men to use their stored-up oil freely on bolt and back-sight-flange. And harassed men, and men ill-furnished, complained bitterly. And men improvising and adventurous slipped away along the traverses, to fetch back brimming mess-tin lids, or salvaged jam tins steaming.

How do you get hot water in this place of all water — all cold water up to the knees. These poured quickly lest it should cool off, and eyed their barrels' bright rifling with a great confidence, and boasted to their envious fellows, and offered them the luke-warm left over. So that one way and another they cleaned their rifles — anyway the oil softened the open cracks in your finger-tips.

While these things were being done, while they were at this oiling and tearing off of closely rationed 'four by two', conserving carefully each flannel slip, plumbing dexterously with weighted cords,[7] scraping and making their complaint, a message reached them from the right for the Lewis Team with No. 8: to get at once on their day-target, to send a man for S.A.A.[8] to Pioneer Keep; further, to furnish a report of their night firing. They stood unhappily, and believed themselves to be ill-fortuned above the common lot, for they had barely slept — and a great cold to gnaw them. Their wet-weighted gear pulled irksomely, soaking cloth impeded all their action, adhered in saturate layers when they stood still.

Night-begotten fear yet left them frail, nor was the waking day much cheer for them. They felt with each moment's more ample light, but a measuring, a nearing only, of the noonday hour — when the nescient trouble comes walking.[9] Their vitality seemed not to extend to the finger-tips nor to enable any precise act; so that to do an exact thing, com-

petently to clean a rifle, to examine and search out intricate
parts, seemed to them an enormity and beyond endurance;
as one, who, clumsied with fear or unnerved by some grief,
seeks to thread needle or turn an exact phrase; for they were
unseasoned, nor inured, not knowing this to be much less
than the beginning of sorrows. They stood as a lost child
stands in his fatigue, and gape-eyed, where tall Guardsmen,
their initiators and instructors, moved leisurely about, well
pleased with the quiet of the sector.

Presently Mr. Jenkins came with Sergeant Snell and they
ported arms for inspection.

He neither blames nor praises,
he whistles low,
he whistles *Dixieland*,
he passes on to Section 4: but
Sergeant Snell checks Jac Jones, checks Jack Float at the ease
springs.[10] Sergeant Snell turns on this going; pokes this right-
middle finger at this lance-jack—
instructs him:
Have ready two on 'em—section's rations.

Sergeant Snell gobs in the trench drain; comes to Mr. Jenkins's heel.

It was yet quite early in the morning, at the time of Satur-
nalia, when men properly are in winter quarters, lighting His
birthday candles—
all a green-o.[11]
When children look with serious eyes on brand-new mir-
acles, and red berry sheen makes a Moses-bush, to mirror in
multiplicity the hearth-stones creature of fire.

But John Ball, posted as 1st Day Sentry, sat on the fire-step;
and looking upward, sees in a cunning glass the image of:
his morning parapets, his breakfast-fire smoke, the twisted
wood beyond.

Across the very quiet of no-man's-land came still some
twittering. He found the wood, visually so near, yet for the
feet forbidden by a great fixed gulf, a sight somehow to
powerfully hold his mind. To the woods of all the world is
this potency—to move the bowels of us.

To groves always men come both to their joys and their undoing. Come lightfoot in heart's ease and school-free; walk
on a leafy holiday with kindred and kind; come perplexedly
with first loves—to tread the tangle frustrated, striking—
bruising the green.

Come on night's fall for ambuscade.

Find harbour with a remnant.

Share with the proscribed their unleavened cake.

Come for sweet princes by malignant interests deprived.

Wait, wait long for—

with the broken men, nest with badger and the marten-cat
till such time as he come again, crying the waste for his
chosen.

Or come in gathering nuts and may;

or run want-wit in a shirt for the queen's unreason.

Beat boys-bush for Robin and Bobin.

Come with Merlin in his madness, for the pity of it; for
the young men reaped like green barley,

for the folly of it.

Seek a way separate and more strait.

Keep date with the genius of the place—come with a weapon or effectual branch—and here this winter copse might
well be special to Diana's Jack, for none might attempt it,
but by perilous bough-plucking.[12]

Draughtsman at Army[13] made note on a blue-print of the
significance of that grove as one of his strong-points; this
wooded rise as the gate of their enemies, a door at whose
splintered posts, Janus-wise emplacements shield an auto-
matic fire.

In the mirror: below the wood, his undulating breastworks all along, he sees and loses, thinks he sees again, grey movement for the grey stillness, where the sand-bag wall dipped a little.

He noted that movement as with half a mind—at two o'clock from the petrol-tin.[14] He is indeterminate of what should be his necessary action. Leave him be on a winter's morning—let him bide. And the long-echoing sniper-shot from down by 'Q' Post alone disturbed his two hours' watching.

His eyes turned again to where the wood thinned to separate broken trees; to where great strippings-off hanged from tenuous fibres swaying, whitened to decay—as swung immolations
for the northern Cybele.
The hanged, the offerant:
  himself to himself
  on the tree.[15]
Whose own,
whose grey war-band, beyond the stapled war-net—
(as grey-banded rodents for a shelving warren—cooped in their complex runnels, where the sea-fret percolates).
Come from outlandish places,
from beyond the world,
from the Hercynian—
they were at breakfast and were cold as he, they too made their dole.[16]

 And one played on an accordion:
    Es ist ein' Ros' entsprungen
    Aus einer Wurzel zart.
Since Boniface once walked in Odin's wood.
 Two men in the traverse mouth-organ'd;
four men took up that song.

> *Casey Jones mounted on his engine*
> *Casey Jones with his orders in his hand.*[17]

Which nearer,
which so rarely insular,
unmade his harmonies,
honouring
this rare and indivisible
New Light
for us,
over the still morning honouring.
This concertina'd
Good news
of these
barbarians,
them
bastard square-heads.[18]
  Put the fluence on,
Rotherhithe—
drownd the bastards on
Christmass Day in the Morning. Wot's this—
wot type's this of bloody waits
wot's this he's striking up—
wot type's this of universall Peace
through Sea and Land.[19]

Mr. Jenkins and his platoon sergeant came again from their
tour of inspection; mired and blue-slimed with liquid mud
from 'P' sap, where No. 4 kept watch in isolation in a night-
digged ditch, dyked between enemy and friend. The two detailed for section's rations silently rose up, together with the
lance-corporal; as silently fell in behind, filed heavy-footed,
disappeared at the earth-work's turn.

The others sat solitary; each one about his own thoughts, except for the two music makers, who, done with their song, discussed the merits of each other's artifice; till these too became silent and wrapped their little instruments in Paisley handkerchiefs against the damp.

Perhaps they found this front-line trench at break of day as fully charged as any chorus-end with hopes and fears; or els their silly thoughts for their fond loves took wing to Southwark Park.[20] Their loves whose burgeoning is finery trickt-out, who go queenly in soiled velveteen, piled puce with the lights' glancing.

The stall-flares' play defines or shades: in the flecked shadow warm cast half lights trace an ample excellence, strings of penny pearls, and jostled grace:

. . . they're two-a-penny, they're orl ripe, they're fresh as daisies dearie . . . and push the barrow home, taking the short-cut, by Jamaica Level.[21]

Certainly they sat curbed, trussed-up, immobile, as men who consider the Nature of Being. Each reflected in the opaque water, each from the oozy margin, and searching comfortward, his weighted feet drew out; as cats by April conduits, mew-up fastidious paws.

From where John Ball sat and did his brother-keeping, mirror-gazing, in the corner of the fire-bay, he could easily observe the dispositions of his companions, and the nature of the place the fully-come day had now exposed, and robbed of mystery.

Billy Crower,
Jack Float,
Tom Thomas,
Siôn Evan,
Jones, rations,
Jones, Mitchell-Troy, with
Lizzie Tallboy, with

Dai de la Cote male taile,[22]
Watcyn, Wastebottom, and the rest,
his friends.

Each one sat silent, all in a row, some smoked, all were mirrored in the leaden water.

Behind each, his rifle leant at an ordered inclination against the parapet. Each bayonet-brightness with sacking veiled, each newly-cleaned bolt and breech-part, similarly, empty sand-bag shielded; and round their legs, and about their necks, like tied amices, were hessian coverings.[23] So quickly had they learned the mode of this locality, what habit best suited this way of life, what most functioned, was to the purpose, and easily obtained.

These went in sackcloth and slept with harness on, which things of accident came to signify the special peril of these parts, became an honourable badge—to blazon in back-areas a front-line Charlie.

Here they sat, his friends, serving their harsh novitiate.

They get certain dispensations with the Guns, the way of life they follow in the A.S.C. is at all times sung in a lay against them.[24] H.Q.-wallahs, Base-wallahs and all Staff-wallahs are canteen-wallahs, who snore-off with the lily-whites; but these sit in the wilderness, pent like lousy rodents all the day long; appointed scape-beasts come to the waste-lands, to grope; to stumble at the margin of familiar things—at the place of separation.

Across a hundred yards or so, where no thing stirred at all above the tangled grass, wind ruffled, sometimes, ever so little, the others too; he stands vicariously, stands aware, stands tensioned within his own place.

And with the night sometimes the dark meeting of these by lot chosen—each the Azazel to each, other daemon drawn to other—[25]

You had no idea he had a patrol out.

The thudding and breath to breath you don't know which way, what way, you count eight of him in a flare-space, you can't find the lane[26]—the one way—you rabbit to and fro, you could cry, you fall in home over, you nestle next '35 Crower, his tiresome questions between your heart drums. You'd like a private hole to go to.

We maintain ascendancy in no-man's-land.

Wastebottom got up and yawned, Watcyn got up and stretched; he felt with his hand between adhering layers of cloth—he announces: Wet bloody through I am—pneumonia it is without any question, congestion for every bugger, piles and disorders of the juices.

Wring your vest man, there is no enemy here.

Veno's, corporal—cures for rough weather.

Rub him front and back—it is Mother Evans's embrocation he wants—indent for embrocation, corporal.

They complained each to each other, they blasphemed the whole order of Being, they hoped breakfast would soon be up.

John Ball remembered the kind Borderer and his outgoing gift—the dry wood left under the fire-step. He felt with his heel as he sat at his sentry work; his eyes still fast on his periscope, pathetically conscientious of his orders—anyway, there was no wood, wet or dry. The casual Guardsman who had come before Stand-to, had evidently seen to other things than the proper disposition of grenade-boxes.

In a little while they came again, the Lance-Corporal with his file of two, carrying a full sack.

No. 1 section gathered, bunched, in the confined traverse; that lance-jack balances carefully his half mess-tin of rum.

They bring for them,
in common:

71

Loose tea mingled with white sugar, tied in heel of sand-bag, pudding fashion, congealed, clinging to the hemp mesh, and one tin of butter.

They bring for them,
for each and for several;
he makes division, he ordains:
three ration biscuits,
one-third part of a loaf,
two Field Service postcards,
one Field Service envelope,
one piece of cheese of uncertain dimension, clammy, pitted with earth and very hairy, imprinted with the sodden hessian's weft and warp; powerfully unappetising;
one tin of *Tickler's* plum and apple for three,
two packets of *Trumpeter* for cigarette smokers,
one tin of issue tobacco for pipe smokers.

They press forward, they speak half audibly or stand aloof. Their mixed round-skulls, long-barrow heads, nobble each. Stratford-atte-Bowe mingles west-tribe modulated high and low, in their complaint.[27]

Yess I hav always, yes, never touch the stuff, no.

Always 'ad fags corporal, always 'av' of.

Seen you with a pipe, Crower.

Not me corporal.

Who are these pipe smokers—'35 Float, you're a pipe man.

Somehows right off it corporal, since they brought us into this place.

'Struth—very well—one packet of *Trumpeter* all round—you whoresons

must we fetch you immaculate *Abdullas* out of this earth.[28]

There is occasions and causes, corporal.

Heave that bull-shit to Jerry, tin and all, for a happy Christmas—it'll gas the sod.

PART 4

Come off it Moses—dole out the issue.
Dispense salvation,
strictly apportion it,
let us taste and see,
let us be renewed,
for christ's sake let us be warm.
O have a care—don't spill the precious
O don't jog his hand—ministering;
do take care.
O please—give the poor bugger elbow room.

There—what did I tell you—can you beat it—have you ever seen such a thing in your life.

Would you bloody-believe-it—some old cows fetch from their bellies proper hobbadehoys.

Is this the blest cruse at Zarephath that you should make so free with it.

Not be a long chalk—
as a matter of fact it's rather a poor issue to begin with —
and—Quartermaster-Sergeant Hughes behind his double blanket
back there
is a Holloway tradesman still.

He learned a trick by water
at Pugh's Hygienic Dairy to the impoverishment of the Lord's people; which technique stands him in good stead, and C.S.M. Tyler, where he is, down in his deep dugout knows how to thrust his flesh-hook and to fill his kettle, cauldron or pot, to make himself fat with the chief offerings.

In the mess they say openly: Paul pinches, Apollos waters —but they're good soldiers the pair of them—proper disciplinarians—yes, by God—and love their men.

Each one in turn, and humbly, receives his meagre benefit. This lance-jack sustains them from his iron spoon; and this is thank-worthy.

Some of them croak involuntary as the spirit's potency gets the throat at unawares.

Each one turns silently, carrying with careful fingers his own daily bread. They go, as good as gold, into the recesses of the place and eat what to each would seem appropriate to breakfast; for that dealing must suffice till tomorrow at this time. You could eat out of their hands.

There was an attempt with tea and sugar. There was fumbling with fire and water and watched-pot.

Fall of trench dampt the fire, fall of fire spilt the water, there are

too many hands to save the boil.

Slow-boy laid hold on calcined dixie-handle—that made him hop—laugh—why, you'd laugh at Fanny.

It was Jack Float, who in the end brought boiled water, borrowed from the next platoon right, tepid with carrying; so that after all after a fashion, they drank their morning tea.

John Ball, relieved for sentry, stood to his breakfast. He felt cheese to be a mistake so early in the morning. The shared bully was to be left in its tin for the main meal; this they decided by common consent. The bread was ill-baked and sodden in transit. There remained the biscuits; there remained the fourth part of a tin of jam; his spoonful of rum had brought him some comfort. He would venture along a bit, he would see Reggie with the Lewis-gunners. He stumbles his path left round traverse and turn.

At the head of the communication trench, by the white board with the map-reference, the corporal of a Vickers team bent over his brazier of charcoal. He offers an enamelled cup, steaming. Private Ball drank intemperately, as a home animal laps its food, not thanking the kind agent of this proffered thing, but in an eager manner of receiving.

74

After a while he said: Thank you sergeant—sorry, corporal
—very much—sorry—thanks, corporal.

He did not reach the Lewis-gunners nor his friend, for
while he yet shared the corporal's tea he heard them calling
down the trench.

All of No. 1 section—R.E. fatigue.

He thanked these round their brazier and turned back
heavy-hearted to leave that fire so soon, for it is difficult to
tell of the great joy he had of that ruddy-bright, that flame-
less fire of coals within its pierced basket, white-glowed, and
very powerfully hot, where the soldiers sat and warmed themselves and waited to see what the new day might bring for them
and him, for he too was one of them, shivering and wretched
at the cock-crow.

Give the poor little sod some char[29]—that's what the corporal had said.

No. 1 section were already moving off, he fell in behind, and
followed on. Slowly they made progress along the traverses,
more easy to negotiate by light of day. Not night-bred fear,
nor dark mystification nor lurking unseen snares any longer
harassed them, but instead, a penetrating tedium, a boredom
that leadened and oppressed, making the spirit quail and tire,
took hold of them, as they went to their first fatigue. The
untidied squalor of the loveless scene spread far horizontally,
imaging unnamed discomfort, sordid and deprived as ill-kept
hen-runs that back on sidings on wet weekdays where waste-
land meets environs and punctured bins ooze canned-meats
discarded, tyres to rot, derelict slow-weathered iron-ware
disintegrates between factory-end and nettle-bed. Sewage
feeds the high grasses and bald clay-crop bears tins and braces,
swollen rat-body turned-turtle to the clear morning.

Men-bundles here and there in ones and twos, in twos and
threes; some eating, others very still, knee to chin trussed,
confined in small dug concavities, wombed of earth, their

rubber-sheets for caul. Others coaxed tiny smouldering fires, balancing precarious mess-tins, anxious-watched to boil. Rain clouds gathered and returned with the day's progression, with the west wind freshening. The south-west wind caught their narrow gullies in enfilade, gusting about every turn of earth-work, lifting dripping ground-sheets, hung to curtain little cubby-holes. All their world shelving, coagulate. Under-earth shorn-up, seeled and propt. Substantial matter guttered and dissolved, sprawled to glaucous insecurity. All sureness metamorphosed, all slippery a place for the children of men, for the fair feet of us to go up and down in.

It was mild for the time of year, what they call a Green Christmas.

They spoke words of recognition where familiar faces poked out from bivvy-sheets, where eyes peered from dark hovel-holes, flimsy-roofed with corrugated-iron. They gained information, in their passing, of the state of the war as it affected 'A' Company, which brought little additional data to their own observations — it appeared to be equally cushy on the whole half-battalion frontage. They passed a point where the fire-trench cut the pavé road, the road of last night's itinerary. They passed where an angled contrivance of breast-works formed a defensive passage, a cunning opening eastward, opening outward, a sally-way; a place of significance to drawers up of schemes, a pin-point of the front-system known to the Staff. They typed its map reference on their orders in quadruplicate. Brigade clerks had heard of it—operators got it over the wire. Runner Meotti ferreted his way with it, pencilled from a message-pad.

Officer's party will go out from X 19 a 9 5 AAA will proceed by drain-course left of road to approx. X 19 b 3 2 AAA will investigate area for suspected enemy works at juncture of Sandy and Sally X 19 b 5 2

Barbed entanglements before this place were doubly strong:

red-coiled mesh spiked above the parapet, armatured with wooden knife-rest stances.[30]

Here were double sentries and a gas guard. Lewis-gunners squat in a confined dark; there was some attempt at an emplacement. Two of them, industrious, were improving their loophole from the inside, to get a widened field of fire. Grey rain swept down torrentially. The water in the trench-drain ran as fast as stream in Nant Honddu in the early months, when you go to get the milk from Pen-y-Maes.

They turned at a sharp angle, right, where it said:

TO PIONEER KEEP

It was better in the communication trench, where slatters[31] had but lately been at work; and planking, freshly sawn, not yet so walked upon nor mired over, but what its joiner-work could, here and there, make quick that delectation of the mind enjoyed with sight of any common deal, white-pared, newly worked by carpenters. Botched, ill-driven, half-bent-over nail heads protrude, where some transverse-piece joint-ed the lengthways, four-inch under-timber, marking where unskilled fatigue-man used his hammer awkwardly, marring the fairness of the thing made—also you trip up on the bleeder, very easily.

Since dawn, no artillery of light or heavy, neither ours nor theirs, had fired even a single round within a square kilometre of the front they held. Down on the right they were at it intermittently, and far away north, if you listened carefully, was always the dull toil of The Salient—troubling—like somebody else's war.[32] At least, the veterans, the know-alls, the wiseacres, the Johnnie Walkers, the Mons angels, tugging their moustaches, would incline their heads.

Wipers again.

He can't keep off it—like a bloke with a pimple.

What's the use of the place anyway—where's the sense
in it.

Don't talk wet.

Who's talking wet.

You're talking wet.

They get warmed to it—they're well away in
tactics and strategy and
the disciplines of the wars—
like so many Alexanders—are perfect in the great commanders names—they use match-ends
to represent
the dispositions of
fosse and countermure.

Who's bin reading *Land and Water*.[33]

Don't nobble Chinese Gordon.

When did they pass you out Hector-boy.

Sheer waste of intelligence—notorious
example of
the man with the missed vocation.

G.S.O. 1—thet's his ticket—the Little Corporal to a turn
—they're bringing up his baton—wiv the rations.
Wiv knobs on it,
green tabs an' all.
Rose-marie for re-mem-ber-ance.
Green for Intelligence.[34]
Where's yer brass-hat.
Flash yer blue-prints.
Hand him his binocular.

Keep a civil tongue—knew these parts back in '14—before yer milked yer mother.

Not the only bugger—there's Nobby Clark
back at the Transport[35]

reckons he snobbed for 'em at Bloemfontein,
reckons he's a Balaclava baby,
reckons his old par drilled the rookies for
bleedin' Oudenarde,
reckons he'll simply fade away.
They're a milintary house the Clarks—'14,
'14 be buggered—

> Pe-kin
> Lady-smith
> Ashan-tee
> In-ker-man
> Bad-er-jos

Vittoria Ramillies Namur,[36]
thet's the Nobby type o'
battle-honour.

This Dai adjusts his slipping shoulder-straps, wraps close his misfit outsize greatcoat—he articulates his English with an alien care.

   My fathers[37] were with the Black Prinse of Wales
at the passion of
the blind Bohemian king.
They served in these fields,
it is in the histories that you can read it, Corporal—boys
Gower, they were—it is writ down—yes.
   Wot about Methuselum, Taffy?
I was with Abel when his brother found him,
under the green tree.
I built a shit-house for Artaxerxes.^*
I was the spear in Balin's hand
                  that made waste King Pellam's land.

* This letter and those on the five succeeding pages refer to subdivisions of
note 37; see page 207.

I took the smooth stones of the brook,
I was with Saul
playing before him.
I saw him armed like Derfel Gatheren.[B] '
I the fox-run fire
       consuming in the wheat-lands;
and in the standing wheat in Cantium made some attempt to
form— (between dun August oaks their pied bodies darting) [C]
And I the south air, tossed from high projections by his Oli-
fant; (the arid marcher-slopes echoing—
should they lose
Clere Espaigne la bele) .[D]
   I am '62 Socrates, my feet are colder than you think
on this
Potidaean duck-board.[E]
   I the adder in the little bush
whose hibernation-end
undid,
unmade victorious toil: [F]
In ostium fluminis.
At the four actions in regione Linnuis
       by the black waters.
At Bassas in the shallows.
At Cat Coit Celidon.
At Guinnion redoubt, where he carried the Image.
In urbe Legionis.
By the vallum Antonini, at the place of boundaries, at the toil-
ing estuary and strong flow called Tribruit.
By Agned mountain.
On Badon hill, [G] where he bore the Tree.
   I am the Loricated Legions.[H]
Helen Camulodunum is ours;
she's the toast of the Rig'ment,
she is in an especial way our Mediatrix.

PART 4

She's clement and loving, she's Friday's child, she's lov-
ing and giving;
O dulcis
imperatrix.
   Her ample bosom holds:
Pontifex maximus,
Comes Litoris Saxonici,
Comes Britanniarum,
Gwledig,
Bretwalda, as these square-heads say.
   She's the girl with the sparkling eyes,
she's the Bracelet Giver,
she's a regular draw with the labour companies,
whereby
the paved army-paths are hers that grid the island which is
   her dower.
Elen Luyddawg she is—more she is than
Helen Argive.[1]
   My mob digged the outer vallum,
we furnished picquets;
we staked trip-wire as a precaution at
Troy Novaunt.[1]
   I saw the blessèd head set under
               that kept the narrow sea inviolate.
To keep the Land,
to give the yield:
   under the White Tower
               I trowelled the inhuming mortar.
   They learned me well the proportions due—
by water
by sand
by slacked lime.
   I drest the cist—
the beneficent artisans knew well how to keep

the king's head to keep
the land inviolate.

    The Bear of the Island: he broke it in his huge pride, and over-reach of his imperium.
The Island Dragon.
The Bull of Battle
     (this is the third woeful uncovering) .
Let maimed kings lie—let be
O let the guardian head
keep back—bind savage sails, lock the shield-wall, nourish the sowing.
The War Duke
The Director of Toil—
   he burst the balm-cloth, unbricked the barrow
(cruel feet march because of this
              ungainly men sprawl over us) .
O Land!—O Brân lie under.
The chrism'd eye that watches the French-men
that wards under
that keeps us
that brings the furrow-fruit,
keep the land, keep us
keep the islands adjacent.

I marched, sixty thousand and one thousand marched, because of the brightness of Fflur, because of the keeper of promises
        (we came no more again)
who depleted the Island,
        (and this is the first emigrant host)
and the land was bare for our going.
    O blessèd head hold the striplings from the narrow sea.
    I marched, sixty thousand marched who marched for Ky-
nan and Elen because of foreign machinations,

       (we came no more again)
who left the land without harness
       (and this is the second emigrant host).
O Brân confound the counsel of the councillors, O blessèd
head, hold the striplings from the narrow sea.
   In the baized chamber confuse his tongue:
that Lord Agravaine.
He urges with repulsive lips, he counsels: he nets us into expeditionary war.
   O blessèd head hold the striplings from the narrow sea.
   I knew the smart on Branwen's cheek and the turbulence
in Ireland
       (and this was the third grievous blow).ᴷ
   I served Longinus that Dux bat-blind and bent;
the Dandy Xth are my regiment;
who diced
Crown and Mud-hook
under the Tree,
whose Five Sufficient Blossoms
yield for us.
   I kept the boding raven
          from the Dish.
With my long pilum
I beat the crow
from that heavy bough.
   But I held the tunics of these—
I watched them work the terrible embroidery that He put
on.
I heard there, sighing for the Feet so shod.
I saw cock-robin gain
      his rosy breast.
I heard Him cry:
     Apples ben ripe in my gardayne
I saw Him die.ᴸ

I was in Michael's trench when bright Lucifer bulged his
primal salient out.
That caused it,
that upset the joy-cart,
and three parts waste.
    You ought to ask: Why,
what is this,
what's the meaning of this.
Because you don't ask,
although the spear-shaft
drips,
there's neither steading—not a roof-tree.ᴹ
    I am the Single Horn thrusting
by night-stream margin
in Helyon.ᴺ
    Cripes-a-mighty-strike-me-stone-cold—you don't say.
    Where's that birth-mark, young 'un.
    Wot the Melchizzydix! — and still fading — jump to it
Rotherhithe.

> Never die never die
> Never die never die
> Old soljers never die
> Never die never die
> Old soljers never die they never die
> Never die
> Old soljers never die they
> Simply fade away.³⁸

The morning bore all that quiet broken only by single and
solitary action that consorts with wet weather. That kind of
day when kitchen-helps half-open doors in areas, poke pink
hands to hurrying tradesmen: How wet you are Mr. Tho-

roughgoods—a shocking morning for you. And with the door's slam there is nothing in the street at all but rain between the buildings and you settle down to a very wet morning indeed. It keeps everyone who's got one in his snuggery and those unluckier lugged in close-under an improvised lean-to, or anyway against some lee wall.

No. 1 section seemed the only unfortunates stirring. All things were very still, universally wet wrapt; this sodden silence might have been from eternity unchanging, seemed a timeless act of fluid dissolution.

They reached a place where the high walls of the communication trench considerably contracted at a turn, reducing the strip of sky above them. These reeking sack walls block all lateral view, and above, nothing is visible save the rain-filmed, narrowing ribbon of sky.

Men sensitive of hearing cock heads enquiringly, as rodents aware, prick ears, acutely directed suddenly.

The narrow air where they walked, registered in quick succession, a series of distinct, far over, separately discerned, vibrations; and after the drawing of a breath—for the balmy morning, for the damp inertia: delved plungings boring to the root of things.

High-powered, of sure trajectory, that big bugger stopt short, with so oddly insignificant a thud, yet to upheavals of earth and water. The dug place in whose depth they sheltered shockt and tremored with each projectile's violent nosing, whether of dud or lively detonate.

As though that Behemoth stirred from the moist places, tensored his brass sinews suddenly, shattered with deep-bellied trumpetings the long quietude; awaking stench and earthquake in his burrowing-up.

Black chemist's smoke thinned out across the narrow neck of sky. The pandemonium swung more closely, with a 5.9[39] dud immediately outside; cascades of water charged with clods of earth, emptied on them from above. Two shrapnel-bursts high-over, by good fortune fused a little short for such exact alignment, drove hot fumes down to hang in the low place where they waited helplessly, white-faced, and very conscious of their impotence.

Each half-second the fields spout high their yellow waters with a core of flame. For ninety seconds black columns rise—spread acrid nightmare capitals. Corrosive vapours charge their narrow world. Their sack wall tremors—the trench seemed entirely to list and to not recover after that near one—here it bulges nastily.

Small hung-edges, and under-cuts, things just holding, things ripe to fall, crumpled, caved, redistributed their weights, established a fresh sequence of stresses, found a level, —and small gulleys filled, and high projections made low.

They say that when the Boar Trwyth broke the land, by Esgier Oervel, with a fifth part of Ireland; who in his going by destroyed indifferently, men and animals, and the King's son there, Llaesgeven who was good for no one, got off without a scratch, to come safe home again. The ingenious Menw, despite his craft, was a sick man all his life after because of the poisons loosed. The two auxiliaries who were swift and useful were not seen again after that passage, when the quiet came again with the sudden cessation—in the tensioned silence afterwards you couldn't find a rag of them[40]— only someone complaining under a broken revetting-frame.

As they hurried to Pioneer Keep they heard confused calling from the fire-trench and one running up behind shouts as he comes nearer, for bearers.

Bearers at the double.

No, the last burst it was—caught 'em unexpected.

It's Mr. Donne of No. 8 who's got it and Fatty Weavel in the sap and some Staff bloke they can't identify.

What brought him to this type of place, why his immaculate legs should carry him, jodhpurs and all, so far from his proper sphere, you simply can't conceive.

Their progress was without event; here and there the trench was lower built or not so repaired from damage, and they momentarily had view of where a continuing double line of trees masked the passage of a road, parallel to where they went securely in the trench; the road they walked on in the darkness of the night before.

Most of them failed to recognise this landmark and were at a loss as to their position and precise direction, except that they supposed themselves to be making for Sandbag Alley, that long circuitous corridor of last night's gropings. They felt only the maze-likeness of all their goings, being aware of nothing much more than the approximate direction of the enemy line. As when you come toward the sea and are conscious of her, and know vaguely the direction you must take for your eyes to see her, yet are in ignorance of the crooked by-streets to and from the jetty.

You live by faith alright in these parts.

You aren't supported as you spend yourself in this blind doubling on your bleedin' tracks by the bright reason for it, they know about back there.

You know no more than do those hands who squirt cement till siren screams, who are indifferent that they rear an architect's folly; read in the press perhaps the grandeur of the scheme.

Clarence was on that remarkable job.

Dai clickt for that do.

Clarence knows little of the unity for which his hours are docketed—little more than bleating sheep the market of her fleece.

You are moved like beasts are moved from upper field to

87

pound, one hour carrying heaped-on weights, the next you delve in earth, or stand long time in the weather, patiently, a hitch in the arrangements; and now singly, through unfamiliar, narrow, ways. You don't know which high walls enclose your lethal yard, or what this tight entry opens on.

They met no one on their way and said few words to each other. It must have been a quarter of an hour before they halted where a tramway cut the trench. The continuing rain came softly, in even descent, percolating all things through.

A low shelter stood, its galvanised inclining roof reflecting the sky's leaden, resounded to the water-pelter, each corrugation a separate gully, a channel for the flow. The trench-drain, disintegrated, fallen-in before the strong current it was built to canalise. Aquatic suckings betrayed where some tiny trickling found new vent-way for the rising inundation.

The trench tramway went straightly, losing its perspective in the rain-mist, off to the left. This trackway led to a juncture, met another single track, where ill-oiled wheels screech on quiet nights when they bring the ration trucks from Richebourg of the Vow, and fearfully they wonder if he'll hear.

This was a country where men from their first habitation had not to rest, but to always dyke and drain if they would outwit the water, or leave the place to fowl and amphibious beasts. It was a bad country to contend in, when such contention most required a way of life below the ground. Yet by fascined track they come to within their walls. They labour with the bulging gabions, they ladle and wattle: like Ewein, they are familiar with the path of a water-course;[41] they make conduits, they divert and block and restore the breaches. Two armies face and hold their crumbling *limites* intact. They're worthy of an intelligent song for all the stupidity of their contest. A boast for the dyke keepers, for the march wardens.

Lance-Corporal Lewis looked about him and on all this liquid action.

It may be remembered Seithenin and the desolated can-trefs, the sixteen fortified places, the great cry of the sea, above the sigh of Gwyddno when his entrenchments stove in. Anyway he kept the joke to himself for there was none to share it in that company, for although Watcyn knew every-thing about the Neath fifteen, and could sing *Sospan Fach* to make the traverse ring, he might have been an Englishman when it came to matters near to Aneirin's heart. For Wat-cyn was innocent of his descent from Aeneas, was unaware of Geoffrey Arthur and his cooked histories, or Twm Shon Catti for the matter of that—which pained his lance-corporal friend, for whom Troy still burned, and sleeping kings re-turn, and wild men might yet stir from Mawddwy secrecies. And he who will not come again from his reconnaissance—they've searched his breeches well, they've given him an ivy crown—ein llyw olaf—whose wounds they do bleed by day and by night in December wood.[42]

Lance-Corporal Lewis fed on these things.

Corporal Quilter made investigation round and about the lean-to. No human being was visible in the trench or on the open track. A man, seemingly native to the place, a little thick man, swathed with sacking, a limp, saturated bandolier thrown over one shoulder and with no other accoutrements, gorgeted in woollen Balaclava, groped out from between two tottering corrugated uprights, his great moustaches beaded with condensation under his nose. Thickly greaved with mud so that his boots and puttees and sandbag tie-ons were become one whole of trickling ochre. His minute pipe had its smoking bowl turned inversely. He spoke slowly. He told the corporal that this was where shovels were usually drawn for any fatigue in the supports.[43] He slipped back quickly, with a certain animal caution, into his hole; to almost immediately poke out his wool-work head, to ask if anyone had the time of day or could spare him some dark shag or a picture-paper. Further, should they meet a white dog in the trench her name was Belle, and he would like to catch any bastard giving this Belle the boot.

John Ball told him the time of day.

No one had any dark shag.

No one had a picture-paper.

They certainly would be kind to the bitch, Belle. They'd give her half their iron rations—Jesus—they'd let her bite their backsides without a murmur.

He draws-to the sacking curtain over his lair.

Corporal Quilter beckoned his men to where a series of disused fire-bays led from the main trench.

Picks, shovels, dredging-ladles, carriers, containers, gas-rattles, two of Mrs. Thingumajig's patent gas-dispersing flappers, emptied S.A.A. boxes, grenade boxes, two bales of revetting-wire, pine stakes; rusted-to-bright-orange barbed wire of curious design—three coils of it; fine good new dark efficient corkscrew staples, splayed-out all ways; three drums of whale oil, the splintered stock of a Mauser rifle, two unexploded yellow-ochre toffee-apples, their strong rods unrusted; three left-leg gum-boots; a Scotch officer's fine bright bonnet; some type of broken pump, its rubber slack punctured, coiled like a dead slime-beast, reared its brass nozzle out from under rum-jar and picket-maul.[44]

This trove piled haphazardly, half-submerged. You must have a lumber room where you have habitation.

Corporal Quilter calls the leading man. He indicates with a jerk of the head the job of work.

One and one, from one pair of hands to another equally reluctant, they pass the shovels the length of the file.

Corporal Quilter stands watching.

There wanted one shovel to the number of the party. Private Saunders devised that he should be the unprovided man, by the expedient of busying himself with his left puttee, conveniently come down.

Corporal Quilter spits from time to time on the duckboard. He hands to Private Saunders a dredging-ladle and the heavier pick, the other he takes himself. He gives the word of command to move on.

The warden of stores withdraws again his curtain; his shiny thread-bare hind-parts first thrust out—now his whole hair-suit torso, now his aboriginal mask.

N.C.O. in charge of party—you corporal.

Corporal Quilter signatures the chit.

12 shovels

2 picks

1 ladle.

See yer bring 'em again—all the so-called complement.

They watched him vanish, mandrill fashion, into his enclosure. They wondered how long a time it took to become so knit with the texture of this country-side, so germane to the stuff about, so moulded by, made proper to, the special environment dictated by a stationary war.

Another ten minutes brought them to a double forking of earthworks. Here they recrossed the road, sharp right; a single barricade of sandbags rose direct from the stone sets to afford some meagre shield. There was no parados, and as they filed over, each man turned his head toward the left, toward

north west, a toward-home glancing, back down the broken
avenue.

Extending fields spread flatly, far to either side, uninter-
rupted to the sight, not any longer barriered nor revetted in.
It was a great goodness in their eyes, this expanse, they drank
in this visual freedom gladly, and were disposed to linger before dropping one by one-down, where Sandbag Alley meets
the road on the north-east side. With that descending this
gate to their prison-house of earth closed-to, which had momentarily stood ajar, tantalisingly upon the western escape,
where the way led back by the forward batteries—to Hen's
Post where you roost in comparative shelter, to Curzon Post
where the support platoon take off their boots by day and
sleep like rajahs on a palliasse, if things pan out reasonably.
To the reserves, to billets, to buildings two stories high, yet
roofed intact—and further still to steadings where the mules
fidget in their lines and make their palaeolithic cries against
the distant flares. To where rosy orderlies smooth the coats
of mares they groom as leisurely as boys in Barsetshire. To
the very marches of the forward zone, to where mess-cater-
ers write their bogus chits. Where once a day, perhaps, the
pickled pilchards jostle the Gentleman's Relish on the top
shelf, with the vibration. Where Frenchmen's children are
at play about the steep weed-grown incline of a '14 Johnson
hole, and each other casement shows its grubby paste-board:

BIÈRE
EGG CHIP 3 FRANC
CAFÉ AU LAIT
ENGLISH SPOKE HEER

And Corporal Bardolph stays and stays.

And beyond again — recedes green kilometre; flat, neat,

Hobbema-scape — but the contours and the pressure vary when you reach
Ste. Marie Cappel.
It's healthy O it's pleasant to be, in
Clairmarais.

After which are places known only by report.
To here they come by day from Whitehall, and sky-blue foederati from The Province, starred, gold-faced, wreathed with silver bay — talk through interpreters. And gorget-patches blaze in their variety, but
O christ the blanco,
O the visitations O—so they say.
They drift up with these Songs of Arcady from time to time.

The zones aren't really water-tight you know.

Sometimes in quiet areas when the morning's aired, they do appear—immaculate, bright-greaved ambassadors, to the spirits in prison; who sip their starry nectar from nickel flasks at noon.

They knock their briars out on their bright *talaria*. They grace the trench like wall-flowers, for an hour; as spirits lightly come from many mansions, and the avenues, where they sit below the pseudo-Fragonards cross-legged, slacked, or lie at night under a Baroque cupidon, guiding the campaign.
After that there is only the Big Ship.[45]

To all this then the road led back, without deviation from Sandbag Alley; which does excuse their dawdling feet.

The same stenches, remembered from the darkness, impurified the heavy air, in and around these deep decaying ramparts. Bobby Saunders felt his last-night sickness wretchedly return, an added misery to his melting bowels. His pick and long ladle tangle with his rifle slung. They let him drop to the rear to find a tumbled, antique, wattled-bay to be alone in.

He was back again, fallen in at the tail of the file. Sallow as

Christmas clown, pink lidded, a skimpy woodbine stuck to his bleached under-lip, irregularly burned, its glow as ruby sequin-shine—worn wryly on goosey flesh on thrashed circus-child.

No party wanted here corporal.

The sapper, workmanly, and with deliberate care, scrapes quite bright his turned shovel-blade.

Just packing up, corporal, bin getting this bit clear since stand-down, better see the gaffer — a bit along be the piss-house next the Gas-post—most like.

They sagged on their digging gear. The freshly-spread chloride threw upward pallid light as Jack Frost would, and unexpected facets tell. This searching unfamiliar influence cast new pallor, and when they looked from each to each they seemed to each a very ghastly crew.

Corporal Quilter comes again. He spits on the slats. He lights a cigarette.

Wash out—'bout turn, lead on back.
Move on, the leading man
lead on in front,
lead on out.

The storeman found the complement correct. In half an hour they were back in the fire-trench traverses.

Corporal Quilter gave them no formal dismissal, nor did he enquire further what duties his party might next perform. Each one of them disposed himself in some part of their few yards of trench, and for an hour or more were left quite undisturbed, to each his own business. To talk together of the morning's affairs; to fall easily to sleep; to search for some personally possessed thing, wedged tightly between articles drawn from the Quartermaster; to re-read yet again the last arrived letter; to see if the insistent water were penetrated within the stout valise canvas, sufficiently to make useless the very thing you could do with; to look at illustrations in last week's limp and soiled *Graphic*, of Christmas preparations with the Fleet, and full-page portraits of the High Command; to be assured that the spirit of the troops is excellent, that the nation proceeds confidently in its knowledge of victory, that Miss Ashwell would perform before all ranks, that land-girls stamp like girls in Luna.

The two Joneses were in argument.

Private Ball groped in his pack to find his book. The India paper was abominably adhered, especially for split finger-tips —and one anthology is as bad as a library and there is no new thing under the sun.

> *Takis, on the motheris breast sowkand,*
> *The babe full of benignitie :—*
>
>   .   .   .   .
>
> *He takis the campion in the stour,*
>
>   .   .   .   .
>
> *He has tane Rowll of Aberdene,*
> *And gentill Rowll of Corstorphine ;*
> *Two better fallowis did no man see :—*

He closed the book—he would eat some chocolate.

Aneirin Lewis sat motionless in the far corner of the bay. The man from Rotherhithe looked to the well-being of his mouth-organ. Private Watcyn was trying to read the scores on the reverse side of Private Thomas's *Western Mail*—as do men in railway carriages. Bobby Saunders slept.

The midday quietness was quite unbroken. They changed sentries at five minutes to the hour, and even this was done without a word for the 'relief' or the 'relieved', regardless of proper usage. A faulty detonated 4.2 deranged the picketed wire outside the trench as the new sentry took over, making him hug closer the parapet, in expectation; but the capricious gunners let be at that, for their ways are inscrutable.

The day wore on without any happening. The sun unseen reached his low meridian. They ate what bread remained from breakfast and opened tins of beef, and more successfully made some tea. The feebleness of before-noon abated, gave place to an after-lunch content. With the passing hours the wind backed from south to south-east to east. Men sneezed, it grew noticeably colder. The sentry at the Gas Post put up the Alert notice. They were almost eager when required to fill sandbags to repair a freshly destroyed defence. They warmed to their work, and found some interest in this remaking. They strengthened their hands like the builders at the water-gate, and everyone wore his harness and so builded other than the watcher[46] at the fire-step, who saw mirrored a new influence break the topmost headers of his parapets; and creep down that dun hostile wall and bathe the rusted tangle of his outer belt—now sweep all the waste with horizontal beam.

Hidden since the dawn he shines at his departing: fretted like captive-fire at boundary-mound. Each interstice burned between lath and common rafter—each cranny bright, where four walls yet held precariously, purlin and principal, far away over, beyond the parados, in the west.

Tomorrow, before daybreak, a ranging heavy will find the foundations and leave the kitchen flooring pounded like red-pepper, with Cecile's school satchel still hanging at its peg; and the Papal Blessing punctured in its gimcrack frame, poking from the midden. Ober-Leutnant Müller will be blamed for failing to locate a British battery.

The watcher at the fire-step began to hope that his friends would so make an end of their work as to spread their tea-napery of news-sheets, to make the dixie boil to synchronise with his relief.

The last direct radiance gave out, his wire and rising glacis

went cold and unillumined, yet clearly defined, in an evenly
distributed after-visibility. The cratered earth, of all grow-
ing things bereaved, bore that uncreaturely impressiveness of
telescope-observed bodies—where even pterodactyl would
feel the place unfriendly.

His mates came from the building-up, and work of restor-
ation; the watched dixie almost boiled. Watcyn had already
opened the *Dairymaid* canned butter, it was just light enough
to know the green and gilt of the enamelled tin. It was an ex-
tremely good brand. The light from their gusty culinary flame
began to tell warmly on the nearer surfaces. The walls with
the skeleton roof stood quite black now against an even clearness, and showed for the last time what remained of that unity intended of their builders. The sky overhead looked crisp
as eggshell, wide-domed of porcelain, that suddenly would
fracture to innumerable stars. The thin mud on the fire-steps
slats glistened, sharpened into rime. The up-to-ankle water
became intolerably cold. Two men hasten from the communication trench. They deposit grenade-boxes in a recess used
for that purpose and quickly go away. A young man in a British warm, his fleecy muffler cosy to his ears, enquired if anyone had seen the Liaison Officer from Corps, as one who asks
of the Tube-lift man at Westminster the whereabouts of the
Third Sea Lord. Vacant faces turned to him. He was advised to
try Mr. Jenkins in the sap. He turned again, the way he came.
Sergeant Snell hurried along the trench carrying a Véry-light
pistol; he detailed four men for company rations as he passed.
The man with the loose tea and sugar shook some part of it
from the sack into the boiling water; and as he poured he heard
unmistakable words, nearing, traverse by traverse from the
right.

Mr. Jenkins was back from the sap:
Drink that stuff quickly and stand-to.
He is away again with no other word.

No-man's-land whitened rigid: all its contours silver fili-
greed, as damascened. With the coming dark, ground-mist
creeps back to regain the hollow places; across the rare atmosphere you could hear foreign men cough, and stamp with foreign feet. Things seen precisely just now lost exactness. Biez
wood became only a darker shape uncertainly expressed. Your
eyes begin to strain after escaping definitions. Whether that
picket-iron moved toward or some other fell away, or after
all is it an animate thing just there by the sap-head or only the
slight frosted-sway of suspended wire.

A long way off a machine-gunner seemed as one tuning an
instrument, who strikes the same note quickly, several times,
and now a lower one, singly; while scene-shifters thud and
scrape behind expectant curtaining; and impatient shuffling
of the feet—in the stalls they take out watches with a nervous hand, they can hardly bear it.

Now the fixed-riflemen take notice: it is almost time for
ration-parties to perambulate the road.

The first star tremored: her fragile ray as borne on quivering exsultet-reed. From Gretchen Trench lights begin to rise,
the first to splutter out, ill discharged.

Have you seen grinning boys fumble with points of flame
who blame the taper's damp. At last, one adequately fused,
soars competently up in hurrying challenge, to stand against
that admirable bright, as crystal cut, lit singly to herald the
immediateness of night.

In a quarter of an hour it was quite dark.

You are told to stand-down.

Night-sentries are posted in twos.

Men detailed are to report at once.

Messages drift from bay to bay.

Pass it along—Mr. Prys-Picton's patrol will go out at 8.30
from Pope's Nose and will return by the Sally-Port. Sentries
will not fire in this area.

PART 4

The countersign is 'Harlequin'.

The Lewis-team by the road are experimenting through their newly enlarged loop-hole.

Fans of orange light broke in dancing sequence beyond his lines.

Bursts in groups of four jarred the frosted air with ringing sound.

Brittle discord waft back from the neighbourhood of the Richebourg truckway.

Guns of swift response opened on his back areas. In turn his howitzers coal-boxed the Supports.

So gathered with uneven pulse the night-antiphonal: mortared-canisters careened oblique descent with meteor trail; and men were dumb and held their breath for this, as for no thing other.

In the next sector the continued vibrating developed greater weight.

High signal-flares shot up to agitate the starred serenity: red and green and white.[47]

The N.C.O. at the Gas Post looked to his apparatus, and placed in a convenient sequence his ready rocket-gear.

But it peters out; and with the lull they speak to each other.

The sentries stand more erect.

They whistle, softly.

Solitary star-shells toss as the dark deepens.

Mr. Prys-Picton's patrol came in, well before midnight.

PART 5

SQUAT GARLANDS FOR WHITE KNIGHTS

He has brought us to a bright fire and
to a white fresh floor-hide.

PART 5

Roll on Duration—

we're drawing pith-helmets for the Macedonian war—they camel-corps wont have platoon drill anyway—deux grenadine ma'm'selle an one beer—this is mine, Alphonso—here's the lucky Alphonse, the genuine lionheart, back in time for the 'bus to Jaffa and the Blackamoor delectations.[2]

He swayed his pelvis like a corner-boy.
A half-platoon in chorus can
fa re barbarously:

> *He shall die*
> *he shall die*
>> *with one*
> *mighty swipe I*
> *will I will*
> *diss-lo-cate his bloody jaw.*[3]

He reverts to the discipline of prose.

Who's kidding—and shorts as well—you ask Sid Whiting at the gum-boot store, straight from the 'major he said—to-morrow we go in again—no—on the left, 'B's' in the craters you bet, it's 'A's' turn by rights—it's the Minnies what gets you down—yes, Ducks Bill, same as where old Snell went sick from—they say the swinger's[4] posted to another mob—we shall lament his going from us, and miss his angel voice an all and show our legs to another.

At the table by the door Private Ball's companion put down Mr. Garvin's last Wednesday's article.

There's time for another one—wont you. We shall be in it alright—it's in conjunction with the Frogs. The Farrier's bloke reckons we move south after this turn on the round-abouts — he got it from the Mobile Veterinary, and there's talk of us going up tonight—no—this 'ere night of all—not tomorrow night my ducky—they've tampered with the natural law—same bit of line, but Supports—how they pile it on—exigenced out of our full bonza, same as last time.

Another takes up the complaint.

Would you be-bloody-lieve it, chastised wiv effin scorpiongs—*o my*,

> *I want-er go home*
> *I want to go over the foam*

I want the Big Ship.
I want Big Willie's luv-ly daughter.[5]
We all want the Man Hanged.

Cold air, driven in, distributes in an unexpected way the wreathed tobacco smoke, and the man with the tablets stands under the lintels, the bane-bearer, who disturbs our piping times.

In half an hour, 'B'—in all your bridal clobber—he's waiting on you.

That's torn it, make it a quarter, can't you.

You will dump packs in ten minutes at the Q.M.'s; and the estaminet is quickly emptied, leaving only Jacques, to sip his coffee, as he had done, since the Fall of the Commune.

The Medical Officer's orderly brought with him the smell of iodine from the room behind the bar.

Bon swores cheriee.

She said good night good *voyage* good fortune from the good God—and finger-tipt renewal here and there; straightened this canted hob-iron; and began immediately to collect the glasses.

He went out, like the others, through the glass door. More putty gave away with the slam-to.

In three quarters of an hour they passed, making the shutters rattle. She could see their efficient looking iron hats, between where the taped curtains nearly met at the middle pane; in fourfold recession, subtly elliptical, each one tilted variously yet in a strict alignment, like pegs on a rigid string. Words of command lost shape against the sealed windows; the beam of light from her oil lamp shone on them through the glass, shined on cleaned numerals, and on the piling-swivels of rifles slung.

She counted to herself, her rounded elbows lifted, as Boucher liked them, held within the action—she put down the glass, half-wiped: forty-four sections of four across the ray, not counting odd bobbing ones and twos who hurry after— that was more than last time; she had wondered for these newer ones, in their ill-filled-out tunics, who crowded with the others and drank *citron*, who were silent as she passed between the tables, who would dangle their bonnets.

The other companies followed at their proper interval, singing, through the May night shower:

> *We dont want ham*
> *lamb or jam—we dont want*
> *roly-po—ly*.[6]

She settled to her glass-wiping. Jacques took his coffee nearer the *Aisne* stove,[7] and when he spat it sizzled on the heated iron.

The company cookers came in the rear—the swaying gadgets knock—as they had done every fourteen days, with hardly a break for three months past; before that they were billeted further up, and were relieved less often.

She bolted the door for the night
and when it was morning
Jacques said that the Englishman's guns had kept him awake.

She said that it was a pleasant morning, and the first in June.

He said it was time the English advanced, that they were a stupid race, anyhow.

She said they were not.

He would like to remind her of the *Pastoral*,
for which she laughed a long time,
with: Vah, vah,
and her head wagging
with: *La—la la*, and her finger pointed, with:
Tawny-tooth go watch the priest, and:
Bent-wit.[8]

She said that the war was lucrative, and chid him feed the
fowl, and smoothed her pinafore: sometimes the Siege Artillery came in during the morning, if there wasn't a shoot on.

They came out to rest after the usual spell. The raid had been
quite successful; an identification had been secured of the
regiment opposite, and one wounded prisoner, who died on
his way down; '75 Thomas, and another, were missing; Mr.
Rhys and the new sergeant were left on his wire; you could
see them plainly, hung like rag-merchants' stock, when the
light was favourable; but on the second night after, Mr. Jenkins's patrol watched his bearers lift them beyond their parapets. Private Watcyn was recommended for a decoration, and
given a stripe; the Commanding Officer received a congratu-
latory message through the usual channels.

They crowded in of evenings: another Draft arrived, and Fatty Weavel with them, back from his Blighty-one already.

Jacques sat at his coffee when they moved off again, out of
Reserve, into the craters, and when they came again to Reserve, out of the craters, he still sat so. Private Whiting, in
his cellar, by candle light, sorted and paired again, checking
the complement correct, of returned gum-boots; putting
aside the less punctured ones for favoured intimates of his;
considered to himself what congenial job a man might wangle
for Mesopotamian nights: You must be pretty fly with these

moves in the air, or get returned to Company in the general shuffle. Mr. Jenkins got his full lieutenancy on his twenty-first birthday, and a parcel from Fortnum and Mason; he grieved for his friend, Talbot Rhys, and felt an indifference to the spring offensive—and why was non-conforming Captain Gwyn so stuffy about the trebled whisky chits.

On Sunday:
they fell out the fancy religions;[9] the three Jews were told off for fatigue at the latrines. Mr. Jenkins was detailed to march the R.C.s four kilometres to the next village to mass; because of Father Larkin being up at the Aid Post, with his Washbourne *Rituale*, and the saving Oils.

The official service was held in the field; there they had spreaded a Union Jack on piled biscuit tins, behind the 8 in. siege, whose regular discharges made quite inaudible the careful artistry of the prayers he read.

He preached from the Matthew text, of how He cares for us above the sparrows. The medical officer undid, and did up again, the fastener of his left glove, behind his back, throughout the whole discourse. They sang *Onward Christian Soldiers* for the closing hymn.

In the afternoon: blown whistles terminate the game before the close of the first half.

It's the four-fold shrill call,[10] it's: *All Companies*. It bodes an equal poise with that racket developing on the left.

. . . and see how they run, the juniors in muddied drawers, who hurry to quarters. The Orderly Sergeant of 'B' kicks back his afterlunch blankets — he is away, he breaks their Sabbath calm with urgent and explicit words.

The field is emptied; and within the huts the reluctant haste, and clumsy-fingered assembling of parts, and:

What's to do sergeant.

What order sergeant.

Is it a fatigue sergeant.

Sergeant me goggles are torn.[11]

Sergeant, '73 or '79 Jones, sergeant — Lance-Corporal Lewis wants to know sergeant.

And is he the Lord Haig to divine the times and the hour, is he, with three up, Selfridge and Gawd-a'-Mighty to provide for them — is he creeping Jesus to search the secret counsels—do the square-heads privilege him with operation orders—is he Von Kluck's fancy lady—whistle for yer daring Daniels, if you want to know the writing on the wall — but wontcher listen to the Band—if you have ears at all attuned, hear the unmistakable development from Cherry-Garden Post to the Mole-hole,

from the Moated Grange

from Mulberry Bush Fosse

from Keep 14,

from Jocks Redoubt

and more frantically from Dogs Alley—and brokenly from the troubled isolations, from the tumuli of the Forward Zone: the beating of hollow brass, and horns keening, as if outlandish men, with imitative magic would steal his thunder—and the Divisional Siren acknowledges.[12]

You stand by in billets and complain, for more than an hour, trussed up and girded, but at tea-time counterpointing violences give the thing a new twist, the plain cadence modulates ominously — breaks all remembered records—he cuts the painter properly—flames uncontrol over the whole subsector. This nasty type of flamboyance makes you light another cigarette from the stub-end of the one before—makes Fatty sing loudly of the Armentieres lady—makes '79 Jones, in his far corner, rearrange and arrange again a pattern of match-ends.

Each variously averts his perceptions, masks the inward abysm; and Sergeant Ryan watches from the open door the signs in the evening sky.

You suppose the texture of his soul to inform the dark and exact contour his buff coating describes against the convulsed cones of light; he would seem of one piece with his slanted iron hat-rim—he who is an amiable cuckold—yet how should we his True Love know, we on whom he turns his rigid heel, at whom he barks, to bloody well fall-in — Jump on these fag-ends!

They were paraded and moved without numbering off; they were marched five kilometres without halting, to reach the Support Posts as the bombardment became negligible; they were back before the *estaminet* closed, but were confined to billets for the remainder of the evening.

Night passed, and the new day came quite quietly; three hostile mines had cratered no-man's-land; he had put over gas, but the wind was fickle, the gunners had responded accurately to the S.O.S.

He had failed to occupy.

Corporal Watcyn was reduced for being not present, and drunk, at the Stand-to parade.

Private Watcyn celebrated his return to the ranks with some of his immediate friends; he concluded the evening in a quarrel with Alice, over the negotiability in the *Nord* of notes issued by the *Pas-de-Calais* authorities.

The Parade was at 8 o'clock for the Divisional baths; they marched lightly, in 'clean fatigue.'[13] The rubbed sore skin, here & there, about the body, pained almost pleasantly, freed from constricting webbing, thigh-bones worked easily at their articulation; not feeling with each movement, the regular

chafe of water-bottle carrier, nor entrenching-tool haft—
bruising, going on bruising, however much you re-adjusted
the brasses[14] — and there was a comfort to have huckaback
tucked round your neck, and everybody talking a lot, and
the day warm, like going to the sea; and away from, a little
further from the line with each unputteed step—and Mr.
Jenkins would strike at midge-flies with his cane, and forget
a bit about Talbot Rhys and laugh at the screaming Froggy
brats by the fresh-painted white uprights of the canal bridge,
where you break-step and go over like a rabble, which apparent messiness is none the less prudently ordered. The worst
of it is, you're lousy again in a day or so—the stuff they use
dont really touch the eggs.

There is a wiring fatigue to be supplied for Back Area
Defences; Nos. 6 and 7 click as usual, and move off with the
unexpended portion.[15] It isn't so bad, it's a bit of luck he's
feeling indifferent to—the Allied Cause.

He gave them a long rest for lunch, sitting in the June sun;
and the grassy bank with million daisies spangled, and buttercup sheen made warm upward glint on piled arms; like Win-
nall Down, behind Miss Best's teetotal hut; and drinks at the
estaminet afterwards. They dropped a couple of unused coils
in the stream; and not anyone the wiser; and packed up at
4.30; to be back in time for 'A' company's concert outside
The Dry.[16] C.S.M. Trotter sang *Thora* for his second encore;
the long Wykehamist subaltern posted to 'D', from the last
Draft, and co-opted for the evening, looked sad for the score
they put before him; but their applause filled the night and the
orchard, where the piano was set up.

There was a Kit Inspection in orders for Wednesday and Gas
Drill at the Divisional School; 'buses for that, either 'buses
or: There's a bloke here going sick—with short-arm parade
after tea an all you wont getter the boozer till eight at the

soonest it's a typical rest cure joint and place of recuperation
and happy lands for war-weary heroes—that's where a foot-
mob has jam on it and adequate refreshment between each
tour in.

It was about an hour after Lights-out, and he caught the horse
lines, and Nobby's shop too, which sent up half the company's boot repairs; No. 7 was turned out to get water from
the pond—the tell-tale flames intrigued his observation posts;
long-distance shells crawled from far over, like interminable
rolling stock; the siege-people woke up; a cantankerous liveliness disturbed the hovering dark; out of this June half-night
neighing horses reared on you, trailed their snapt tethering,
cantered off; and dark hoof-thudding, circles concentrically
the heavy fields, and clods thrown high—these dumb, who
seem to sense how they perish with this flesh—their whinnying so pitiable.

You weren't back in kip till two, and at two-thirty anti-air-
craft blokes Pom-pom vertically, fleck woolly puff-balls, to
counter-flower, where the bright beam-searching piles; and
the sable field is punctured bright, an incredible height up;
razor-splinters soar down from the stillness, after the last
burst, and altogether in the oddest fashion, killing Alice's best
layer, and the C.O.'s mare.

Everybody said the battalion route march for tomorrow
would be cancelled, but it wasn't: he rode the adjutant's
dapple-grey.

They went in again, unexpectedly, the same evening, which
was a Friday, because the boxing match, with Mr. Hague in
the ring against Taffy Hopkins, fixed for Saturday night, was
scratched.

'B' supplied carrying parties for the Show; but at zero

minus five minutes, exactly on the frontage of attack, his fore-stalling barrage clamped down—and you knew where to put Operation Orders.

In the packed assembly-trench they still waited, drest to the battle and nowhere to go, their synchronised watches as fatuous as last year's almanac; and every artery, to or from, unnegotiable; and every telephonist with a dead instrument about his ears.

They came out next evening, and discussed the High Command at Alice's.

Good luck to him anyway—properly nipped in the bleed-ing bud, properly nobbled—not one of our mob copped it—would you believe it with all that muck flying—they reckon they want to draw his attention up this way, the real thing is going to be down south.

Maybe, but that dont explain how he taped this do to such a nicety—wide—'struth—I should say.

John Ball's companion contributed his theory: Put wide I shouldn't wonder—one of these Staff toffs tipt him the wink—half these brass-hat swells are uncommonly reminiscent of goose-step merchant with a false moustache.

Thet's right Marmaduke—thet's hit it—lose your iden'ity on a pre-war milintary mission.

The man from Rotherhithe sipped very gravely, his abomi-nable beer; sometimes he held his slowly emptying glass to the light; when he replaced it on the marble, he did so with-out the faintest audibility. He looked straight-eyed and level-ly; through bunched heads, through the Sacred Heart, done in wools, through the wall, through the Traffic Control no-tice, on the board, outside, opposite; through all barriers, making as though they are not, all things foreign and unloved; through all things other and separate; through all other things to where the mahogany cornices of *The Paradise*—to the saw-

dust thinly spread . . . the turned spirals that support the
frosted panes they call through, half-open, from the other
bar, is a good job o' work. . . . Nat West put that in when
they enlarged the house; he got the wood cheap when they
broke up *The Golden Vanity*—at the Royal Albert, in the
cholera year. . . . Surrey Commercial stevedores call drinks
for the Reykjavik mate . . . she's lying across the water and
goes out tonight . . . she's bound for the Skagerrak with
plant from Ravenhills.[17]

And Alice moved among the tables with her tray.

He said, without any motion at all: They'd pour piss like
this down plug-hole in a self-respecting turn-out.

With half an inclination toward his companion:

Another one cock? . . . two more miss.

Pushed across the spilled-on flat, small coin—his eyes still
level with the needlework on the wall:

What about Alice here—dont trust the Frogs—yer body
or yer dough, ev-er-ry time—remember the white mare at
Ler-ven-tee in '15;[18] dont trust any on 'em.

Corporal Lewis used his hands in emphasis; the man from
Rotherhithe quietly drew his glass to safety.

I tell you your contentions is without reason, it is indeed
a normality in the vicissitudes of the blutty wars—moreover
his Intelligences is admirable, the most notorious in all the
world.

Thets it Corp, stand be our little piece—bring us another,
Alice, and deux citron—(but who is this at the lattice—
there's no mistaking his ugly footfall)—and one vin blonk,
sweet chuck, to placate the bastard—urge lenity wiv a spot
of the ordinaire.

But he has put on, with his side-arms,
incorruptibility,
he is aloof;

they are unlucky;
his pencil is taken slowly down from behind his grocer's ear
—the sight of his cropped head inflames your uncharity.

Here comes bloody Anti-Christ with a packet for each us'n's.
Sheep nor goats dont signify, cries
John o' the Dale
          (Harry of Ilkley is gone without his hat).
He is licking the indelible stub-end—he chooses without distinction of person:
You an' you an' you an' you and smart to it—draw 'em at the Quarter's an' two blankets.
Frayed-edged Army Book slips back to tunic's right bottom pocket, with the button left unfastened.
My party—fall in outside.
And the door's closing brings freedom for their tongues.
          (Private Henry Earnshaw returns for his service-
          cap.)
T'boogger's sharp eyed—bah mal fay[19]—yon's wick as Swale-side rat
—and sidles out to make No. 4 ont' billeting party.
They hear the voice of the taskmaster: Double up thet man double up thet man—move them long York loins o' yorn
—I'm no Griselda.

Getting pretty much of a wait and see sort of mob these days—he's having a really nice time with his book o' life and yous and yous and not-ter-reason-why technics—it used to be fourteen in and five out regular—knew where you were — everything conducted humane and reasonable — it all went west with the tin-hat — that harbinger of their anabasis, of these latter days, of a more purposed hate, and the establishing of unquestioned ascendancy in no-man's-land — and breaking his morale and—this new type of toffee-apple, and these very latest winged-pigs,[20] whose baleful snouts rend up no mean apocalypse, and the mk. IX improved pattern of bleedin' frightfulness.

Why not parade the Jolly Tars and Jack's the boy — we could do with a silent diver's mate, we could do with a tin fish to shift him up in the Islands,[21] and that Rooshun roller wants more juice—whereas we lie checkmated and their theory of attrition is a mug's game—he puts the heavy stuff over and we establish a definite superiority in the neighbour-hood of the Brick-stacks—by a typical ruse he entered our forward posts in the Richebourg sector—but was easily ejec-ted—his strong attempt astride the Menin Road is most gal-lantly repulsed—and potentates come up to Montycats[22]— 'Tis some poor fellow's skull says he—Christ have mercy!

Orl right, cock—so called Duration—what you signed for.

The Orderly Room runner pushed in among them, with their interrogating eyes.

It's a stone ginger[23]—to-morrow.

'Buses? — no — first smokers— Pullman and all — corner seats for corporals—bastard Southern Belle boy—billeting-party shoved off to-night—war starts Thursday 2.30 ac em-ma official—they're falling out the undertakers.
Get combed-out with the coffin makers.
I heard say he were a ship's carpenter, sergeant, he's with No. 8, sergeant.

They waved to her where she opened the shutters to the early sun; advanced-parties of the Bedfords were already standing about, and strange faces looked out from familiar openings; they joined 'C' and 'D' at the cross-roads, and so formed, for the last time, by the Lys River, and turned from the dyked meads, and from

PART 5

Pecantin
le Plantin
Cats Post
Dogs Post
Rags Post
Bones Post
Mole hole Keep
Croix Barbée

Gorre of the sheltering coppice that you come to from the
Islands; or when they relieve you in Ducks Bill, where his con-
cavities is sufficient;[24] and some of you come alive from the
unquiet hill whose eruptions smoulder under each cold lip
of clay; and conflagrations change the shape of the sky; and in
the morning that mountain is removed that he may work his
evils easily in your immediate rear; and last night's demonstration brings him so near, you can hear his sentries breathe.

When you come from this waste your tongue is not loosed
till you're past Cuinchy lock, and you come with the tow-
path into a green peace; and Gorre is that peace, beyond le
Plantin marsh, small, with its little wood, and the sound of
dredging.
You will remember it joyously
who remember dolorously, 'H' and 'K' saps.

And these were sad, who marched, who thought of green
Gorre.

And so from Reiz Bailleul they came, and the place called
Paradis they left on the left; and through Lestrem, to a large
uncomfortable town, and away in the morning.

They billeted warm that night, in plentiful hay, freshly carried; you could lie, with exquisite contentment, and listen
to the war.

They moved off early, to avoid the hottest sun, in country

that only remembered Uhlan patrols, in the standing crops of '14.

Where tiny hills begin at last to bring you from the Flaundrish flats, they rested, two days. In a meadow place, like our Queen Camel, they swimmed in streams, and washed their cootied shirts; and white Artois geese would squawk, and sway a wide-beamed femininity between the drying garments spreaded out. Officers in slacks walked the village street in the cool of the evening. Private Ball had a satisfactory parcel from his aunt in Norwood; people spoke lightly to each other as they do on fine mornings in England, when the prospect pleases them—and they will insist it's such a lovely day—and Evelyn's operation is next Wednesday at eleven; Alex reckons it's not so serious, but old Mrs. Pennyfather wags her ex-professional finger—she's seen too much of that sort of thing. And so has Old Sweat Mulligan. He admits we've come on as to guns, anyhow quantitatively, but where's the musketry of '14—and what will these civvy cissies make of open country and how should Fred Karno's army know how—to take proper advantage of cover.
He wails like a minor prophet
he gets properly worked up
he would like to know, Lord God he would
where's the discipline
requisite to an offensive action.

Down behind low walls at the further end of the village, man in black walked between his vegetable beds; he handled his small black book as children do their favourite dolls, who would impute to them a certain personality; he seemed to speak to the turned leaves, and to get his answer.

The south-east wind came to sway his beanstalks, to mingle with the drone of bees, a heavier burden.

Private Ball loitered at the wall, where he passed on his

fatigue, with Private Thomas . . . to watch the lips move beneath the beaver's shade, where a canonical wiseness conserved in an old man's mumbling, the validity of material things, and the resurrection of this flesh.[25]

The south-east murmuring insisted on recognition; he poked his book away in the skirts of his soutane.

Allemands—no bon—eh?

They tried to tell him it was British gunfire; that the war would soon be over—but he paid no heed.

Allemands—beaucoup de bombardment—plenty blessés.

He turned between where the bees hived, between low plants, to his presbytery.

It was a good idea not wearing tunics for the march, but a bit chilly to start with, and if you're a Skinny Lizzie, it's best to put a sock under the shoulder-straps.

Why cant the limbers carry the packs, there's stacks of room; some of them manage to dump their's with their bloke's valises—or anyway get their personal extras, knocked-off oddments, and spare comforts, tucked away with the official baggage.

You feel the pack of the Ox-blood Kid—it's as light as the Rig'mentals—there's a whole lot of them that work it: the Pox-Doctor's Clerk, for one, the chitties, and types of scullion bummers up, specialist details, all of Caesar's household, chlorination Daniel, Private Miles who warms the Old Man's water.[26]

(But among them, his dark ribbon hardly shows on the fouled khaki, for spattered-up kitchen greases, his ladylike dial as sooted as when he essayed the Boars Head Sap, and brought in the great Pomeranian, to cold earth grovelling—and blackened men ran between the falling stars.
He's with his longe ladel
        to test the jippo

he goes with this rout like
            the worshipful Beaumains
the turner of broches
the broth-wallah.[27])
—but they'll soon nark that contriving—they cant abide the
sight of you
unlist yer liker beast o' burden.

The south road gleamed scorching white its wide-plotted
curve; you couldn't see the turned tail of the column, for the
hot dust, by ten o'clock.

    That was the longest day so far and 'B's' billets were a mile
further on—that was thirty kilometres altogether, not counting the bit from Company parade, to the Battalion assembly
point.

The length of the sick parade put the M.O.'s back up—and
what's the use of M.D. with broken blisters.[28]

    Reveille was at 4.30 again next day; there was chalk be-
neath the turf where they lay at the third fall-out; and once
they halted to let pass at a cross-roads a Regiment of another
Division, moving convergent to their line of march; they drew
to the right of the road for tractored howitzers, their camou-
flage-paint blistering at noon-day; you could see the cared-for
working-parts, glistening from under, in deep shadow, the
thrown tarpaulin, heavy on the outside with white deposit; a
lorry with aeroplane parts, and more artillery—for the mag-
netic South

Under a uniformly brazen sky, animals, like winded runners,
choose the narrow shade of north-east facing walls.

They came to billets in a straggling place, whose steep, single street ran in such fashion as to bear all that summer day the full beat down of the summer sun; and now at mid-afternoon, wall and roof, and baked, tilled patches, running back their burning corrugations, slumbered drowsily, sprawled on chalky gradient. The leading company sweltered in, broke their siesta with renewing bugles.

Toward sundown a leadenness spread up from under the world, capricious winds rose and stirred, whirled the three-weeks gathered dust like Punic sands; cockerels became restive on their dung heaps, and splayed their feathers' soiled white—the mastiff-bitch jangled her chain.

When John Ball wakened in the darkness, across the storm mechanised lumbering shook pegged-up accoutrements and the household crockery, with heavy going on the south road; and southward too, the sky flickered uncertainly, as when the summer lightnings dance, and apprehensive sheep scatter to some shelter that they know.

No Battalion Orders had been posted for the day. The wild - ness of the night was abated, but there was the chill that comes after; it yet rained in spasms, and doors slammed before sudden drives of wind—you could really have done with a fire. People stood about in greatcoats, as they stand in bath-wraps at the turning of the stair, and in the draught at junctures, and indeterminate carrying has chilled the shaving water; discussing the validity of the portents, chain-smoke away the eleventh hour, ask naively of trivialities, coax the subject to zoology—perhaps he too heard, last night, the lion roar in the Capitol. Do the strong guts of Sergeant Ryan register the signs—does he sense in his iron bowels how withered are the yew-trees of his country, could he too retch up his heart at this whispering of fixed-stars frighted; of how it's at our very

doors, Dai Davies and the Sibyl do agree—and they reckon
we're in the first wave, for sure.[29]

Father Martin Larkin has opened his canteen, which connotes
some respite.

Father Martin Larkin is available to all ranks between 3.30
and 5.0; that's where the Dagoes slip fatigue—that's not so
healthy, that conforms to the general trend. When Bomber
Mulligan & Runner Meotti approach the appointed channels
you can count on an apocalypse, you can wait on exceptional
frightfulness—it will be him and you in an open place, he will
look into your face; fear will so condition you that you each
will pale for the other, and in one another you will hate your
own flesh. Your fair natures will be so disguised that the aspect of his eyes will pry like deep-sea horrors divers see,
from the portage of his rigid type of gas-bag—but more like
you'll get it in the assembly-trench—without so much as a
glimpse of his port and crest.

At midday they were paraded in fatigue-dress.

After you've numbered-off you can wait ten minutes in the
driven rain.

He threw away his cigarette when he turned the corner;
he acknowledged Sergeant Quilter's salute, and stood them
easy.

You could see some of 'A' company formed before their
billets higher up the road, so it was some business of more
general significance than a platoon fatigue or even a Company
Quartermaster's noonday frolic.

But he carried a jellygraphed sheet and turned to them as
they do on *Excita Quæsumus* Sunday, when he spreads the pastoral on the pulpit rest and they sniff expectantly, or blow

their noses before he starts . . . and Mrs. Callahan prays for
the dead and Mr. Meadows considers the handsome price of
the six silver-gilt—and she the ladder in her stocking. It'll
be the same old tale, venerable brothers, it'll be an heartfelt
appeal to each and every of us—it is no mean thing to uphold
—and there are potent words:

Albuhera, Oudenarde, Malplaquet, Minden; where the
hound's coat mired, and the white mane tangled;[30] and from
Brigade Orders of the 3rd as to proper care of feet; and
under the same date—against the practice of removing stiffening from service caps and from Army as from the 21.6.16,
cancellation of leave, all ranks—like you shan't have that de-
lectable hour I promised you last week come Michaelmas.

He is asking Private Saunders if it is essential for him to
shuffle his feet when he stands easy; he wants to know why
Private Watcyn has such interest in No. 3 platoon, also to do
up the top button of his tunic, and to remember to indent for
numerals—and he waits now, become pernickety.

Sergeant Quilter is fresh from his promotion.

Staandstill in the rearank—cantcher—and eyes to front all
of you.

Mr. Jenkins has begun his précis of the official text.

Received from extract from issued G.H.Q. of the 2nd to
be communicated to all ranks. With transport on the paved
other road you missed half the good news . . . and have carried his trenches on a wide front . . . in the south subsector . . . our advanced troops have penetrated to his third
system. He raises his voice against the crying of the drivers
and there is noise of stress at the bend to disrupt the tale of:
his full retirement—the number of his élite gone to Divisional Cage—and other ranks like the sea-sand taken—field-
howitzers and seventy-sevens running to three figures.

. . . of all calibre in our hands . . . have everywhere been
reached according to plan . . . and are in readiness to co-op-

erate with the infantry. The G.O.C. 444th Corps would take the occasion—but the four-ton changing gear by the traffic-wallah obliterated altogether his expressions of hearty appreciation.

They were permitted to cheer.

You are dismissed, to clean up billets.

The hot spell once broken seemed as remote as last year—they fell in after dark, greatcoats folded outside packs, ground sheets worn. The rain came against their faces, and after the first mile you got uncomfortably hot under the rubber sheeting and with the halt you cooled and shivered; people didn't talk much, & there was little sound at all, but what the weather made, when the feet marching, shuffled to a standstill. The gunfire from the south-east had become for them so normal an accompaniment as to be no longer noted, its cadences unheeded; but at the second halt you began to enquire of this new stillness on the night. Perhaps it was because of the lie of the land, or perhaps he'd beat it right out of hearing, or perhaps this lull were a space between, a breather for them. At all events, the wind bore no sound, other than itself, across the drenched land; or if that changing light as on each other night, danced, for a gunned piping, this hill's bulk kept you uncertain.

But soon, you only but half-heard words of command, and your body conformed to these bodies about, and you slept upright, where these marched, because of the balm of this shower, of the darkness, of the measure of the beat of feet in unison.

It roused your apprehension that the third halt should so exceed the allowed five minutes; and what with the word passed down for the adjutant, and with Brigade cyclists about at this hour, you gathered they were up to their antics—you

weren't surprised when you found yourself facing the way
you'd come:

The brave old Duke of York—up it and down it again.

And the first beginnings of light cold on them by the time
they were back in yesterday's billets; and men so tried chatter overwroughtly, & blame the management, till sleep holds
them, freed from their care, or the cares of Company Quartermaster-Sergeant Higgins, who has no sleep at all, considerate
of these new-fangled states,[31] what make a man spit blood;
bolt upright in his straw, as fated Brunswick in the niche, with
ears wide for the distant drum-fire:[32]

Worst 'un first Wipers—be a long chalk.

They let them lie till ten o'clock, and in the afternoon
moved off again by the other road; at every crossing of
ways, and convenient for carrying, they were piling it up
for him.

The weather had improved a lot.

Fair-dressed young men about the hangar-stays
                    (heaven itself would hasten to the south sky).
Break throttle on you sudden, just over;
disturb the immediate air at the take-off,
bring you on the napper you'd think, bearing so low
over the long column
getting up the fluence
making the four horsemen speak comfortable words, and
smooth her tossing manes; her black-beauty quivering.

Barely clear the poplar top
at cant and obliquely
as Baroque attending angels surprise you with their air-
worthiness — but fleet, with struts braced, to mote in the
blueness, to discover his dispositions, (his grey succours darkening in the neighbourhood of the two Bazentins) noseout
scurry, in his Back Areas.

Troops moved out of the village as their foremost platoons moved in; and during the night a whole Brigade passed through; and very early an artillery advanced-party allocated No. 7's billet to the gun-team of a heavy battery: they found the chalked-up initials when they awakened—the Corps mark was altogether unfamiliar to them.

. . ; packs will be dumped at a convenient hour by company arrangement together with . . . must see that all men . . .

Private 21679, Map. 6 pla. 'B' Coy. temp. att. H.Q. Coy. (office) pending present operations, key-fingered out the long roster of weapons to be borne and the last particular for the specialist details
for the chosen fire-eaters
for the co-opted runners
for the flank bombers with
their respective loads.

And for the born leaders,
the top boys
the hero's grave squad
the Elect
the wooden-cross Dicks
—for the White-men with Emergency Archie: all these types are catered for, but they must know exactly how to behave.

One thousand a hundred and one unicorn horns for a pride of lions
twelve spare mauls for the consolidators,
with a note for Mr. Wogan-Powis to choose his carriers with consideration. Will Mr. Talbot see that his party are properly supplied with gloves; and the auxiliary Bearers should be powerfully bodied and will report to the M.O., on Battn. arr. —but will continue to ration on their respective Companies.

And then there are these other:

the rifle strength
the essential foot-mob, the platoon wallahs, the small men
who permanently are with their sections, who have no quali-
fications, who look out surprisedly from a confusion of gear,
who endure all things:

like Private Dunn, whose bungled puttees clothe his vari-
cose; and the suet-faced Kelly, who, even Staff Sergeant Bale
couldn't make to soldier, yet who is useful enough in a sap-
head
or bringing up the Toffee Apples
or to fetch and carry for
the *Sturm Abteilung*.

The pallid under-aged from Mare Street, East 8, with these
sheep-keepers from the Gwentian hinterland, who heard the
deacon's word, who come to the Lord's battle; these can delve
out the broken men, who know so well the careful salvaging
of this year's young of the flock, when white March piles on
Darren yr Esgob,

(the helpless wethers will only stand by, agape at you, like
an awkward squad; barge in under, to avoid the worst of it)
but they all will carry
250 rds. S.A.A.
with
all available picks and shovels to those
not allotted other accessories.

His fingers moved more rapidly—after all, it's better than
the Company.

He nearly overlooked the rescript from Thursday's orders,
in his desire to satisfy. N.B. Uniformity of practice re ground-
sheets with F.O.;[33] these will be folded on top of the haver-
sack, not underneath, the over-lap will not exceed two inches.

The Signals Officer passed through to the partitioned-off
space behind the curtain of grey blanket, and came again, almost immediately:

PART 5

From Brigade—Aunty Bembridge wants a reply, she's getting fearfully worked up—and forty-eight hours before the balloon rises.

He continued to stenograph:
Operation Orders. Part II.

The buzzer, all the time, tapt out its urgencies, level with his left ear; with only the grey, sagged cloth between, which would bulge toward, when the new operator, posted from the Cheshires, got fussed because the line wasn't clear. Outside, across the yard, the dozen H.Q. details bunched to cast lots with:

> Old Johnny Fairplay all the way from Bombay
> to have a little bit on the lucky Mud-hook[34]

but Post-Corporal Howells stood apart, with her by the pump, and she pied freshly for the afternoon, and wasn't half nice with her small apron-strings tied.

In five minutes he drew out the fair copies. The Adjutant's batman came clumsily with his tray so that the transferred Cheshire man complained bitterly for the deranged wires.

Private W. Map brooded over the tape.

That syphon's cool release let drive in him a reflex kick for the prick, and when all's done and said there are an amenity or two making bearable their high stations—that's why their wives have puddings and pies.[35]

But it really was a thirsty afternoon, and the burdened air at 3.45 allowed no flicker of a featherweight, so that the paper pinned, adhered, a sharp white rectangle above the tied-down pump-tail, sealing an authorised *verboten*.[36]

He heard the emptied tumbler against the table-face, and the sound of papers gathered up, and the acting adjutant's ash tapt, and Orderly Room Sergeant Cherbury's shout for,
Runner Herne
where he lay sunned outside

where he lay like Romany kral
reposing and rook-hair disordered
like fleet-foot messengers would sleep
on windy plains
         who waked rosy-cheek
remembering those deep-bosomed—to worry eyes with
screwed fists.

    Runner Runner Run-nerr!

    Goddam—not tomorrow, hairy Herne—spring to it—
there's a sod of a war on.

    The Outlandish men have to be warned—
the confederates, brother.[37]
'A' and 'C' are halfway to Meaulte*
and the slingers
who muck-in
And the selected ones—an ecclesia who have special meats
—off the Q.M., (they rumour in the Companies) are further
afield still, beyond the medium T.M.'s. You're nearly at Brigade Boundary there, you can see the tents of the Horse-
Marines—who wait to co-operate.

    Who waking, stift searching limb, like Signorelli's Inno-
cent
to rise and shine for
Ares bellowing,
who straightened his tunic, and came in.

    All Companies.

    Yes sir.

    And Regimental Sergeant-Major Bollander.

    Yes sir.

    Find the Reg'mental first.

    Yes sir.

    And this for the Bombing Officer is urgent.

    Yes sir.

            * To be pronounced Me-oult.

You know his billet.

Yes sir.

By the Stokes people.[38]

Yes sir.

He doesn't raise his eyes from the paper-litter to acknow-
ledge your salute even, but on your about turn smartly:

Runner Runner!—rapt like a proper marm.

Run-ner.

Yes sir.

This form-master in khaki strokes his nose with the seasoned
bole — waiting for the formula; for the buzzer behind the
blanket to stop
countermanding one seven one five hours
substituting one six five five hours.

Runner.

Yes sir.

Tell 'em not later than 4.55.

Yes sir.

Tell them to note the correction.

Yes sir.

And find first the Reg'mental.

Yes sir.

I want him now.

Yes sir.

I want him now — I want him here now — he ought to be
here now.

Yes sir.

          Where's the sergeant-major
          I know where he is
where's the old squire—he's ben foully murdered
where's Rosy
where's Pendragon
where is his anointed face in
         all time of our necessity

where's King Scrounger and the man wat knows the ropes—
he's General Weston's pure gold, he's Hur, and that other,
all in one, he's adjuvant and prop to the captains of the host
—he never dies, he simply fades away.[39]

He's already positioned the near pedal with his free instep.
    They call their wins to Bank
and beat about him too, who
                     cries over his right shoulder his annunciation:
    It's twins—and doing well.
    But let's have it the Marathon kid—cut it out, Mr. Mercury
Mystagogue.
    Straight from the mare's mouth and the long trail awinds
at 4.55 prompt, to the Dead March in esses Paul and all—and
get down to affixing the mark at:
T. Atkins hereby declares.
    There's neither bond nor free this outing, Greek nor Bul-
garian, even Canteen Charlie
'ill cock his pop-gun
ere the mountings are much older
Sonny Boy
whole outfit going up with a bang, like
Daddy Brock's Bonus.[40]
    Sped nimbly perched: bright *petasos* canted on bonny brow
between the midden and the byre
farm-flutter at the spokes
downy scatters now——to
      cock-a-diddle-dow
to:
                     O my I dont wantter die
                     I want to stay—in my office
                     all day.
Till Sergeant Cherbury warned them to put a sock in it and the
mastiff-bitch growled dangerously, and lifted her great collar

of iron, to see what might so disturb her mid-afternoon
slumber.

And now you Lord Walter Drakes
whose turn was it?
Roll bowl or pitch
you come in stockinged-feet and go aways in
mo-ter cars[41]
like a Coalition Jack Horner.

But he'll burn more than a sheep-cote this journey and founder more than a cock-boat[42] with bad news for London Town;
and where the Mother of Rivers bares her smooth bulk, where
the little hills skip to wasted Gwaelod[43] —where Sabrina rises:
their Rachels weeping by a whitened porch
and for the young men
and for Dai and for Einion
and for Jac Pryse, Jac Pryse plasterer's son.

They moved within the hour, in battle-order, in column
of company where the road cut a face of downland chalk.

And grass-tufts, too, were like they grow on seaward hills
—with small wiry flowers against the white, and with the return of summer's proper way, after the two days storm, blue-
winged butterflies, dance between, flowery bank and your
burnished fore-sight guard, star gayly Adams's dun gear.

After an hour they halted; to move forward with long extended intervals between each platoon, but before they left
their gully, for the wide ridge, they halted again, to advance
by section.

He found the range as 'D' Company's kitchen drew into
dead ground beyond.

Now in this hollow between the hills was their place of ren-
dezvous.

PART 6

PAVILIONS & CAPTAINS OF HUNDREDS

Men went to Catraeth as day dawned: their fears
disturbed their peace.
Men went to Catraeth: free of speech was their
host . . . death's sure meeting place, the goal of
their marching.

And bade him be ready and stuff him and garnish him . . .
and laid a mighty siege about . . . and threw many great engines . . . and shot great guns . . . and great purveyance
was made on both parties.[2]

The terrain of bivouac was dark wrapt; the moon was in her
most diminished quarter.

It was useless trying to sleep with all this trapesing about
—and the more clumsy ones tripping over the pegged-down
ground-sheet, or poking in-under, to ask if you were 'A' Company—or Sergeant Coke of 'C'—or Mr. Talbot's batman.

Besides which there was the heavy battery operating just
beneath the ridge, at a kept interval of minutes, with unnerv-
ing inevitability, as a malign chronometer, ticking off with
each discharge an exactly measured progress toward a certain
and prearranged hour of apocalypse.

Private Saunders lay, one of three, under the low-sagged
vaulting of laced - together bivvy sheets, like a hare's form,
that they had there constructed on the open down.

The whole valley was dotted in roughly ordered lines with
such improvised shelters as men could devise; and here and
there a tent half-heartedly camouflaged, where a commander
sought his sleep—or cursed by candlelight ambiguous countermanding chits. These three of them sucked Mackintosh's
toffee where they lay, and littered the narrow burrow with
tiny grease-proof paper twists. The post-corporal had tossed
him the parcel when he went down to the water-cart.

The 9-inch kept its interval of fire. Then a companion battery opened out with its full complement — and yet lesser
pieces further forward, over the ridge, spread up fans of light
and from the deeper part of the valley, where by day there
seemed nothing other than a stretched tarpaulin and branches
artfully spread, eight bright tongues licked, swift as adder-

fangs darted. The candle-end by the toffee-tin, flickered and went out—they let it be, and watched the relaying flashes play again.

Good show boy an' lying down to it, couldn't beat it at *The Alexandra*.[3]

Fishy he don't put some back.

He's legging it, mate—he's napoo.

Private Saunders felt for the gone-out candle-end.

Let it bide — let's keep the auditorium dark like a pukka gaff.

Innumerable bright stabs from where at sundown only chalk scars whitened empty.

They lay full length sucking their shared confectionery; watched with great wonderment the opening phase of the preparatory bombardment. But because they were very heavy and their limbs comfortably disposed, sleep overtook them one by one.

So through the short summer night they slept on, and their companions of the Line.

But under the chalk ridge worried gunners wrinkled their brows, plotted exact angles and toiled with decimals, emerged from flimsy shelters strewn of greenery with logarithmic tables. And drivers sweat on foot, their tunics cast to ease the final gradient, to give some added purchase to the cumbered limber wheels.

And so on the morn Elias the Captain came.[4]

And the Regimental was getting hourly more severe. He was beginning to speak of *exigencies* and of the *impending action*, which usage he had learned on the Orange River.

They wanted two extra runners at Headquarter Company to be supplied by 'B'. Private Saunders and another were to report at once.

His two mates said he was lucky—anything better than the Company. But they were wretched when he would extricate

his ground-sheet from its place in the construction of the bivvy,[5] which threw their little shelter miserably out of gear.
They told him H.Q. was lousy with ground-sheets. He said
he must be properly dressed or lose the job and get put on the
peg as well most like. They mocked his timidity; and set about
without any cheer, to reconstruct.

For such breakings away and dissolving of comradeship and
token of division are cause of great anguish when men sense
how they stand so perilous and transitory in this world. Bearing the red brassard of his office he ran about the valley to the
commanders with *urgent* or *ordinary* messages.[6] And once he
saw, was ushered in before Aunty Bembridge in her tent—in
council with the captains and the honourable men. He marvelled at the concentration there.

As one long acquainted with misadventure whose life is ordered to discomfort, conscious of his soiled coat's original
meanness of cut and the marks of his servitude, who stands
shyly in a lighted Board-room, who notes their admirable tai-
loring and their laundered shirts; who looking down observes
his cobbled feet defined against their piled floors, who is relieved and breathes more freely as the noiseless door glides
to. He is on the kerb again in the world he knows about.

He tripped at the tent-rope — he recovered himself. The
Brigade Corporal checked him for an unfastened shoulder-
strap. And Fritz was putting nine-point-twos on the nearer
ridge. Farrier-Corporal Shallow was back from his course at
Corps and came to seek his friends for the last time before the
show. He picked his way between the gun positions, round
past the temporary horse-lines and across by where the engineers were working on some mystery of theirs.[7]

Supply-dumps of mushroom uprising piled at every getat-
able bit of ground. Distressed artillery Lieutenant unfolded
sheet 57d S.E. under nose of R.E. major, to ratify with valid
references his claim to a contested plot.

And the noise of carpenters, as though they builded some scaffold for a hanging—hammered hollowly.

After a while he saw men wearing the sewn-on triangle and the sign he sought[8] and he came to 'B' Company's lines. He gave them the latest as he had heard tell of the devising of this battle . . . and in what manner it should be. He said that there was a hell of a stink at Division—so he had heard from the Liaison Officer's groom—as to the ruling of this battle— and the G.S.O. 2 who used to be with the 180th that long bloke and a man of great worship was in an awful pee—this groom's brother Charlie what was a proper crawler and had some posh job back there reckoned he heard this torf he forgot his name came out of ther Gen'ral's and say as how it was going to be a first clarst bollocks and murthering of Christen men and reck- oned how he'd throw in his mit an' be no party to this so- called frontal-attack never for no threat nor entreaty, for now, he says, blubbin' they reckon, is this noble fellowship wholly mischiefed.

Fall of it what fall may said this Big-head.

Alas said this staff-captain.

Ah dam said this staff-major.

Alas alas said Colonel Talabolion.

Anyway it was a cert they were for it to do battle with him to-morn in the plain field.[9] There was some bastard woods as Jerry was sitting tight in and this mob had clickt for the job of asking him to move on — if you please — an' thanks very much indeed, signally obliged to yer, Jerry-boy.

Corporal Shallow said he didn't like the sound of things.

He wished them the best and cushy ones and started back to retrace his steps through the valley of preparation and the ordnance there set out to his work on the dappled mare.

John Ball heard the noise of the carpenters where he squatted to clean his rifle. Which hammering brought him disquiet more than the foreboding gun-fire which gathered intensity with each half-hour. He wished they'd stop that hollow tap-tapping. He'd take a walk. He'd go and find his friend with the Lewis guns. And perhaps Olivier would be there. No orders were out yet, and tea would not yet be up.

These three seldom met except for very brief periods out of the line—at Brigade rest perhaps—or if some accident of billeting threw them near together. These three loved each other, but the routine of their lives made chances of fore-gathering rare. These two with linked arms walked together in a sequestered place above the company lines and found a grassy slope to sit down on. And Signaller Olivier came soon and sat with them. And you feel a bit less windy.

They talked of ordinary things. Of each one's friends at home; those friends unknown to either of the other two. Of the possible duration of the war. Of how they would meet and in what good places afterwards. Of the dissimilar merits of Welshmen and Cockneys. Of the diverse virtues of Regular and Temporary Officers. Of if you'd ever read the books of Mr. Wells. Of the poetry of Rupert Brooke. Of how you really couldn't very well carry more than one book at a time in your pack. Of the losses of the Battalion since they'd come to France. Of the hateful discomfort of having no greatcoats with fighting-order, of how bad this was. Of how everybody ought rightly to have Burberry's, like officers. Of how German knee boots were more proper to trench war than put-tees. Of how privileged Olivier was because he could manage to secrete a few personal belongings along with the signaller's impedimenta. Of how he was known to be a favourite with the Regimental and how he'd feel the draught if he were back with his platoon. Of whether they three would be together for the Duration, and how you hoped so very much indeed. Of captains of thousands and of hundreds, of corporals, of many things. Of the Lloyd George administration, of the Greek,

Venizelos, who Olivier said was important, of whom John
Ball had never previously heard. Of the neutrality of Spain.
Of whether the French nation was nice or nasty. Of whether
anyone would ever get leave and what it would be like if
you did. Of how stripes, stars, chevrons, specialisations, jobs
away from the battalion, and all distinguishing marks were
better resisted for as long as possible. Of how it were best to
take no particular notice, to let the stuff go over you, how it
were wise to lie doggo and to wait the end.

And watched the concentration in the valley.

Where the road switch-backed the nearer slope, tilted,
piled-to-overloading limbers, their checking brakes jammed
down, and pack-beasts splayed their nervous fore-legs—
stiffened to the incline. And where it cut the further hill a
mechanised ambulance climbed up and over, and another
came toward.

Every few minutes thinned-out smoke wreaths spread up
from beyond, to signify the norm of his withdrawing range
and the reluctant ebb of his fire. But now and then a more pre-
suming burst would seem to overreach its mark and plunge
up white rubble this side; for although the tide be most certainly outbound, yet will some local flow, swell in with make-
believe recovery, to flood again the drying shingle and mock
with saucy spray the accuracy of their tide-charts; make brats
too venturesome flop back with belly-full and guardian nurse
girls squeal.

      Amelia's second-best parasol
              sails the raging main;
   her fine fancy's properly split
             she wont see that ever
they cut it a bit too fine
and there was scattering from that maiming all over the shop,
and the wind right up, and two or three lay sidelong on that
hill, and Ginger O'Hara the padre's bloke and O the white

bodies in the trouble. And a great untidiness breaching the neat line of bivvies; and unpiled arms by great violence with rove-off piling swivels.

The Quarter's knocked-off S.R.D.

is blown to buggery,

diluted and far from home,[10]

what won't half get him shirty.

Mules broke amuck across the open ground, where it said no traffic by daylight, just where his last salvo made dark corona for the hill.

Echoes that make you sit up and take notice tumbled to and fro the hollow in emptied hard collapse, quite other than the sustained,

boomed-out

boom-oom, boom-oom

and the felt recoil,

shocked up from the trained muzzles which sway their sylvan masquerade with each discharge.

John Ball and his friends were watching from their grassy knoll.

A certain liveliness.

He's not half so disposed to turn the other cheek as yesterday.

The signaller was rather in the know or anyway his trade gave him ear to the gossip at H.Q.

He's got snug in his new positions and brought up more heavies our people reckoned on that the Second-in-Command on the wire with Brigade and I gathered our strafe hadn't really begun not till two one four o hours I fancy O we shan't do anything for twenty-four hours of course but of course they may change all that—tamper with the menu every five minutes —in fact orderly room has assumed a real Change Alley atmosphere and talk about tenterhooks and all on thorns and how you really don't know from one minute to the next it's a proper shemozzle. You'd hardly credit it—who do you suppose would not first sit down and think if he be able with a half-brigade—and the Reg'mental looks the Major up and down and takes him for a damned Derbyite—Reg'mental's superb but he can't get over the second Boer War.

The Lewis gunner pulled up bits of daisy.
Waiting for the Esses Essses Bubble to go up — is — abitofa sstrain—I reckon.

New dilapidations on the further hill made the other two attend.

He's got the road this time.
Proper crumps.
I wonder if we'll shift him really.
What's the odds.

What bit of line do you fancy for the winter vacation, when this show's petered gently out.

It's now or never they reckon—they all agree to that you know.

This year next year some time then hold Court of Enquiry as to the probable causes contributing to the loss of the War by Land.

Do you suppose
that rows of Field-Marshals
Don Ac Ac Gees,
G Esses O, 1, 2 and 3 and
Ac Ac Q Emma Gees will
fall on their dress-swords.[11]

Our young men shall see visions. 25201 Ball has clicked for the gift of bloody prophecy, what a wheeze—*hara-kiri* parade by Whitehall Gate—with Royal Mary in her ermine stole and all the king's horses, and the Chaplain General.

He wormed about a bit on his stomach to get quite comfortable and looked intently into the eye of a buttercup.

The Chaplain General will explain how it's a Christian act

142

after all. Give 'em burial in Paul's, there will be letters to
The Times saying it should have been the Abbey, of course
always the Abbey—of course—failing
the long mound over the water.

By the way, the C.S.M. of 'D' has laid a wager with the
Reg'mental over this show—stands to snaffle a hundred francs
if the cavalry get going.

Safe as the Waacs dearie, might as well count on the White
Knight or the Great Twin Brothers.

Why not?—I'm all for victory: how—good—it—would
— be.

Castor neck on Pollux in harness on the right—boot to boot
to Aunty Bembridge with her Mafeking V.C.—all in their
battle-bowlers — more preferably with plumes — when we
go over—this Conchy propaganda's no bon for the troops—
hope Jerry puts one on Mecklenburgh Square—instead of fus-
sing patriotic Croydon. He'd have to gas the whole district,
and Golders Green as well, to be efficacious and — half the
B.E.F.—I shouldn't wonder.

And the Lewis gunner uprooting idly with stretched out
arm still lying on his stomach turned his left cheek to the wiry
downland grass and screwed up his right eye.

Why not join the At-trocities Commission sstraight away
—toot sweet—mu-tilate Little Willie—garrotte Mr. Ber-
trand-bloody-Russell with the Union Flag—detail Fr. Vaughan, O.C. Sergeant Instructors—to pr-reach a course of ser-
mons on the Bull Ring to further foster the offensive spirit.[12]

Tea's up 'B' Company.

Roll up—roll up for yer char.

Roll up me lucky lads.

So long—come again soon, don't get nabbed tapping the
Gen'ral's wire—I'd hate to see you shot at dawn.

'B' Company were making a queue about the field kitchen and

each returning to his group of friends between the bivouac lines with their steaming mess-tins.

And after tea it was a summer evening, simply heavenly if it wasn't for the midges and it was odd not having Fatigues or anything much of course you couldn't get far & you couldn't get a wet anyhow and the whole up and down of the valley like proletarian holiday. But engines positioned for the assault and the paraphernalia of the gunners and all that belongs to the preparation toward a general action and corrugated tin shelters and hastily contrived arbours and a place of tabernacles and of no long continuing nor abidingness, yet not by no means haphazard nor prejudicial to good-order.

Well you couldn't go far afield because of the stand-by but blokes came across from 'A' and the other companies to see their friends and people talked a good bit about what the Show was going to be like and were all agog but no one seemed to know anything much as to anything and you got the same served up again garnished with a different twist and emphasis maybe and some would say such and such and others would say the matter stood quite otherwise and there would be a division among them and lily-livered blokes looked awfully unhappy, people you never would expect it of and same the other way the oddest types seemed itching for a set-to quite genuine it would appear but after all who can read or search out the secret places you get a real eye-opener now and then and any subsequent revealing seldom conforms and you misconstrue his apparent noble bearing and grope about in continued misapprehension or can it by any manner of means be that everyone is interiorly in as great misery and unstably set as you are and is the essential unity of mankind chiefly monstrated in this faint-heartness and breeze-right-up aptitude.

Joe Donkin, that never had spoken to anyone since he joined

the Battalion at Divisional Rest[13] in April except to pass the time of day a grave and solitary man whose civvy occupation no one seemed to know about but old Craddock his most near associate — they always managed to get on the same Fatigue and used to sit silent together in the boozer—this Craddock said he knew but wouldn't divulge but said it was a job no decent man need be ashamed on anyway. Joe looked more set up than ever previous and said outright and before them all that this is what he had 'listed for and how he would most certainly avenge his five brethren from the same womb as himself on these miscreant bastard square-heads and sons of bitches who in a '15 show in these parts so he declared had shamefully done four of them to death in some Jock reg'ment it seemed and the youngest of all six was at this same hour when he Joe Donkin sat and spoke with them going near skelington in Jerry concentration camp back there. Private Float joking and unadvised and because of his inherent inability to get the hang of this man's sensitivity said it serves 'em right for 'listing in a crush like that and how the kilties always got it in the neck if they didn't beat it soon enough which they more generally did and got his arse kicked by this Joe who was in no jocund mood but singly resolved and fore-arming himself in the inward man to be the better and more wholly addressed toward this enterprise of making expiation life for life if by any means he might for the gassing before Fricourt on the same day of the four brothers Donkin all good men of their hands. He said as how blood was thicker nor water three times and went off with Private Craddock and no other word to his bothy at the furthest end of the lines.

The other slope was still sun-lighted, but it was getting almost cool on this east-facing hill, and the creeping down and so across so gradually, gathered to itself, minute by minute, the lesser cast-shadows, the little glints and smallnesses, garnered

all these accidents of light within a large lengthened calm.
Very soon the high ridge-line alone caught cast lateral ray. But
for long after that, his shrapnel bursts, away beyond, were
gauffered at their spreading edges with reflected gold. Across
the evening, homing birds, birds of the air with nests cawed
on high above them waiting, and the preparation there. Oddly
stirred winds gusted coolish to your face, that might have
borne things webbed and blind, or the grey owl suddenly. And
some people began settling down for the night or at least to
get a snooze before this talked-of bombardment loosed off to
make it difficult. Some of them were already fallen to sleep,
but the more solicitous disposed themselves in groups and
stood about on that hill, and rather tended to speak in under-
tones as though to not hasten or not disturb, to not activate
too soon the immense potential empoweredness — and talk
about impending dooms—it fair gets you in the guts.

Let 'em kip on now and take their rest.

But they roused them now and platoon commanders came
—and orderly sergeants with orders and orderly corporals
with some final detail and runners countermanding last minute
memoranda. And bivvies all go down and unlacing of ground-
sheets and each one very concerned with his own affairs and
spreading out things on the earth, and rolling up tightly and
making last adjustments and—what bastard's knocked-off
me trenching-tool-blade-carrier.

They eat whatever cannot conveniently be taken.

They ate John Ball's seed-cake.

Standing together already trussed-up in battle-order with
two extra bandoliers slung, and rifles in their hands—in haste
they ate it.

And crumbs go down between your webbing—but better
carry it in belly than leave it.

He managed to get the tin of sardines into his tunic's left
bottom pocket, along with the two grenades.

Just like them — they issued four apiece just when you gathered you'd everything neatly arranged

In fumbling and haste they did these things.

It was the beginning of the darkness and they moved toward the further ridge.

Now they moved, all the four companies, each platoon at fifty yards' interval. On either side their line of march the waiting batteries.

No. 7 had begun to feel the pull of the incline and No. 6 were coping with the steepest bit, and the leading files of 'A' Company's most advanced platoon already had such sight as the July half-light would allow, of the place beyond—whose bodies knew already the relaxation of the further descent. It was exactly 9.39 by John Ball's luminous wrist-watch when it happened.

It was not so much that the noise surprised you—although you had to spit in a bloke's ear to make any impression.

They spent some hours of that night failing to get contact with the unit to be relieved, but before day broke, No. 7 occupied a shallow trench, freshly digged. They put out wire. It commenced to rain.

Hour on hour the gunfire did not relax nor lessen, in fact took on a more tremendous depth.

Rain clouds thickened to wintry dark across the summer night, broke a soaker over them, more confused them where some sought with inutile trenching tools to deepen against his retaliatory fire. Or some just curled up and chanced it.

No one seemed to know the dispositions of the place but Sergeant Quilter was of the opinion that his platoon occupied a bit of the new advanced line. In this he felt some satisfaction. Mr. Jenkins seemed not to be existent. But soon he re-appears —he says that no one has the foggiest notion who is where.

147

He urges an improvement for their meagre cover.
He digs himself.

When daylight fully came they were withdrawn across the open, which seemed silly, and he obviously saw them and put across Woolly-Bears[14] low over them scampering like disturbed game.

And now you seemed to be in some foreign awfully well made place engineered deep in the gleaming chalk. And the sun stood burning straight above the lie of this trench when the rain stopped and you felt faint for the noisomeness sweated up from the white walls, and all the odds and ends lying about were so newfangle and by the hands of strange men and how is a man to know the habits of their God, whether He smites suddenly or withholds, if you mishandle the things set apart, the objects of His people He is jealous of. You sit with circumspection and you rise with care. And black script inscription at different junctions pointed. And all the arrangements of the place like somebody else's house. The late occupants seem respectable enough by their appointments and certainly one up on the kind of life you've had any experience of for some while. Everything well done and convenient electric light fittings. Cosy, too, and nothing gimcrack and everything of the best. You hope they haven't left any infernal and exactly-timed machines for you before they legged it.

God knows what it was all about, but they moved you back again that evening to another field of bivouac.

And you saw the whole depth of the advance and gauged the nature of the contest yard by yard, and made some estimate of the expenditure and how they'd bargained for each hundred feet with Shylock batteries. You marked how meshed intricacies of wire and cunning nest had played sharp tricks on green and eager plaintiffs. They lay heaped for this bloody suing.

Back past the broken village on the hill — gleamed white inner-plaster where the apse bared in cross section its engineered masonry, which great shearing away and deeps displaying only more made shine out from victim stone the intellection of the builders. For here were blasted bare the opportune thrust, the lively interior contriving, the bright bones of the thing. And the grave-yard huddled—silver black and filigree Mary-Helps and the funerary glass shivered where they ask of your charity. And the civvy dead who died in the Lord with *Libera nos* and full observance, churned and shockt from rest all out-harrowed and higgledy-piggledy along with those other—wood white with heavy script for mortuary monument, for these shovelled just into surface soil like dog— with perhaps an *Our Father* said if it was extra quiet.

But all the old women in Bavaria are busy with their novenas, you bet your life, and don't sleep lest the watch should fail, nor weave for the wire might trip his darling feet and the dead Karl might not come home.

Nor spill the pitcher at the well—he told Josef how slippery it was out there.
O clemens, O pia and
turn all out of alignment the English guns amen.[16]

And mules died: their tough clipt hides that have a homely texture flayed horridly to make you weep, sunk in their servility of chain and leather. There had been only time to shove them just out of the road.

They lay with little sleep one more night in bivouac and went again next day to that bewilderment of white-worked fosse and gallery, artful traverse, and well-planned shelter, that had been his Front System.

And in the afternoon rain, saw, for the first time, infantry go forward to assault.

No. 7 were disposed in high overlooking ground. So that

John Ball & the rest could comfortably, and in cover, because of the run of their trench, observe, as cockaded men of privilege were used to do, who pointed with their batons where the low smoke went before the forming squadrons on a plain. They wondered for each long stretched line going so leisurely down the slope and up again, strained eyes to catch last glimpses where the creeping smoke-screen gathered each orderly deployment within itself. They wondered for the fate of each tenuous assumption—settled back to their immediate duties in the trench. As sea-board men, who watch some perilous outgoing dip to a shrouded speck; who come down from the white sea-wall, turn eyes from the white in-swell and get down to some job of work.

Some time during the night they were moved by a guide into their own assembly positions.

PART 7

THE FIVE UNMISTAKABLE MARKS

Gododdin I demand thy support.
It is our duty to sing: a meeting
place has been found.

PART 7

Invenimus eum in campis silvae
and under every green tree.
Matribus suis dixerunt: ubi est triticum et vinum? Cum defi-
cerent quasi vulnerati . . . cum exhalarent animas suas in
sinu matrum suarum.[2]

The memory lets escape what is over and above—
as spilled bitterness, unmeasured, poured-out,
and again drenched down—demoniac-pouring:
who grins who pours to fill flood and super-flow insensately,
pint-pot—from milliard-quart measure.

In the Little Hours they sing the Song of Degrees
and of the coals that lie waste.
Soul pass through torrent
and the whole situation is intolerable.[3]

He found him all gone to pieces and not pulling himself together nor making the best of things. When they found him his
friends came on him in the secluded fire-bay who miserably
wept for the pity of it all and for the things shortly to come to
pass and no hills to cover us.

You really can't behave like this in the face of the enemy and
you see Cousin Dicky doesn't cry nor any of this nonsense—
why, he ate his jam-puff when they came to take Tiger away
—and getting an awfully good job in the Indian Civil.

After a while he got his stuff reasonably assembled, and '45
Williams was awfully decent, and wipe every tear, and solidi-
fied eau-de-cologne was just the thing so that you couldn't
really tell, & doubled along back, with the beginnings of dawn
pale on the chalky deep protected way, where it led out to
the sunken road, and the rest of the platoon belly-hugged the

high embankment going up steep into thin mist at past four
o'clock of a fine summer morning.
In regions of air above the trajectory zone, the birds
chattering heard for all the drum-fire,
counter the malice of the engines.

But he made them a little lower than the angels and their
inventions are according to right reason even if you don't
approve the end to which they proceed; so that there was
rectitude even in this, which the mind perceived at this moment of weakest flesh and all the world shrunken to a point
of fear that has affinity I suppose, to that state of deprivation
predicate of souls forfeit of their final end, who nevertheless know a good thing when they see it.

But four o'clock is an impossible hour in any case.
    They shook out into a single line and each inclined his body
to the slope to wait.
And this is the manner of their waiting:
Those happy who had borne the yoke
who kept their peace
and these other in a like condemnation
to the place of a skull.

Immediately behind where Private 25201 Ball pressed his body
to the earth and the white chalk womb to mother him,
                Colonel Dell presumed to welcome
some other, come out of the brumous morning
at leisure and well-dressed and all at ease
as thriving on the nitrous air.
Well Dell!
    and into it they slide . . . of the admirable salads of Mrs.
Curtis-Smythe: they fall for her in Poona, and its worth one's
while—but the comrade close next you screamed so after the

last salvo that it was impossible to catch any more the burthen
of this white-man talk.

And the place of their waiting a long burrow,
in the chalk a cutting, and steep clift—
but all but too shallow against his violence.
Like in long-ship, where you flattened face to kelson for the
shock-breaking on brittle pavissed free-board, and the gun-
nel stove, and no care to jettison the dead.

No one to care there for Aneirin Lewis spilled there
who worshipped his ancestors like a Chink
who sleeps in Arthur's lap
who saw Olwen-trefoils some moonlighted night
on precarious slats at Festubert,
on narrow foothold on le Plantin marsh—
more shaved he is to the bare bone than
Yspaddadan Penkawr.
    Properly organised chemists can let make more riving
power than ever Twrch Trwyth;
more blistered he is than painted Troy Towers
and unwholer, limb from limb, than any of them fallen at
Catraeth
or on the seaboard-down, by Salisbury,[4]
and no maker to contrive his funerary song.
    And the little Jew lies next him
cries out for Deborah his bride
and offers for stretcher-bearers
                gifts for their pains
and walnut suites in his delirium
                from Grays Inn Road.

But they already look at their watches and it is zero minus
seven minutes.

Seven minutes to go . . . and seventy times seven times to the minute
this drumming of the diaphragm.
   From deeply inward thumping all through you beating
no peace to be still in
and no one is there not anyone to stop
can't anyone—someone turn off the tap
or won't any one before it snaps.

Racked out to another turn of the screw
the acceleration heightens;
the sensibility of these instruments to register,
fails;
needle dithers disorientate.
The responsive mercury plays laggard to such fevers—you
simply can't take any more in.
And the surfeit of fear steadies to dumb incognition, so that
when they give the order to move upward to align with 'A',
hugged already just under the lip of the acclivity inches below
where his traversing machine-guns perforate to powder
white—
white creature of chalk pounded
and the world crumbled away
and get ready to advance
you have not capacity for added fear only the limbs are leaden
to negotiate the slope and rifles all out of balance, clumsied
with long auxiliary steel
seem five times the regulation weight—
it bitches the aim as well;
                      and we ourselves as those small
cherubs, who trail awkwardly the weapons of the God in
                              Fine Art works.

The returning sun climbed over the hill, to lessen the shad-

ows of small and great things; and registered the minutes to
zero hour. Their saucer hats made dial for his passage: long
thin line of them, virid domes of them,
cut elliptical with light
as cupola on Byzantine wall,
stout turrets to take the shock
and helmets of salvation.
Long side by side lie like friends lie
on daisy-down on warm days
cuddled close down kindly close with the mole
in down and silky rodent,
and if you look more intimately all manner of small creatures,
created-dear things creep about quite comfortably
yet who travail until now
beneath your tin-hat shade.
    He bawls at ear-hole:
Two minutes to go.
    Minutes to excuse me to make excuse.
Responde mihi?[5]
    for surely I must needs try them
so many, much undone
and lose on roundabouts as well and vari-coloured polygram
to love and know
    and we have a little sister
whose breasts will be as towers
and the gilly-flowers will blow next month
below the pound
with Fred Karno billed for *The Holloway*.[6]

He's getting it now more accurately and each salvo brackets
more narrowly and a couple right in, just as 'D' and 'C' are
forming for the second wave.

Wastebottom married a wife on his Draft-leave but the whinnying splinter razored diagonal and mess-tin fragments drove inward and toxined underwear.

He maintained correct alignment with the others, face down, and you never would have guessed.

Perhaps they'll cancel it.
O blow fall out the officers cantcher, like a wet afternoon or the King's Birthday.[7]
Or you read it again many times to see if it will come different:
you can't believe the Cup wont pass from
or they wont make a better show
in the Garden.[8]
Won't someone forbid the banns
or God himself will stay their hands.
It just can't happen in our family
even though a thousand
and ten thousand at thy right hand.

Talacryn doesn't take it like Wastebottom, he leaps up & says he's dead, a-slither down the pale face—his limbs a-girandole at the bottom of the nullah,
but the mechanism slackens, unfed
and he is quite still
which leaves five paces between you and the next live one to the left.

Sidle over a bit toward where '45 Williams, and use all your lungs:

Get ready me china-plate[9]—but he's got it before he can hear you, but it's a cushy one and he relaxes to the morning sun and smilingly, to wait for the bearers.

Some of yer was born wiv jam on it
clicked lucky and favoured

pluckt brand from burning
and my darling from unicorn horn with only a minute to go,
whose wet-nurse cocked a superstitious eye to see his happy
constellation through the panes.

But it isn't like that for the common run and you have no men-
suration gear to plot meandering fortune-graph nor know
whether she were the Dark or the Fair left to the grinding.

Last minute drums its taut millennium out
you can't swallow your spit
and Captain Marlowe yawns a lot
and seconds now our measuring-rods with no Duke Josue
nor conniving God
to stay the Divisional Synchronisation.

So in the fullness of time
        when pallid jurors bring the doomes
        mooring cables swipe slack-end on
barnacled piles,
and the world falls apart at the last to siren screech and
screaming vertical steam in conformity with the Company's
Sailings and up to scheduled time.

As bridal arranged-paraphernalia gets tumbled—eventually
and the night empties of these relatives
if you wait long time enough
and yesterday puts on to-day.
    At the end of the suspense
come the shod feet
hastily or laggard
or delayed—
but anyway, no fretting of watch on the wall nor their hys-
teria,

can hamper nor accelerate
exact kinetics of his advent
nor make less miserable his tale to tell
   and even Mrs. Chandler's tom
will stiffen one Maye Mornynge
to the ninth death.

Tunicled functionaries signify and clear-voiced heralds cry
and leg it to a safe distance:
leave fairway for the Paladins, and Roland throws a kiss—
they've nabbed his batty for the moppers-up
            and Mr. Jenkins takes them over
and don't bunch on the left
for Christ's sake.

            Riders on pale horses loosed
and vials irreparably broken
an' Wat price bleedin' Glory
Glory
Glory Hallelujah
and the Royal Welsh sing:
Jesu
            lover of me soul . . . to *Aberystwyth*.
But that was on the right with
the genuine Taffies
            but we are rash levied
from Islington and Hackney
and the purlieus of Walworth
flashers from Surbiton
men of the stock of Abraham
from Bromley-by-Bow
Anglo-Welsh from Queens Ferry
rosary-wallahs from Pembrey Dock
lighterman with a Norway darling

from Greenland Stairs[10]
and two lovers from Ebury Bridge,
Bates and Coldpepper
that men called the Lily-white boys.
Fowler from Harrow and the House who'd lost his way into
this crush who was gotten in a parsonage on a maye.
Dynamite Dawes the old 'un
and Diamond Phelps his batty[11]
from Santiago del Estero
and Bulawayo respectively,
both learned in ballistics
              and wasted on a line-mob.

Of young gentlemen wearing the Flash,
from reputable marcher houses
with mountain-squireen first-borns
prince-pedigreed
from Meirionedd and Cyfeiliog.
C. of E. on enlistment eyes grey with mark above left nipple
probably Goidelic from length of femur.
Heirs also of tin-plate lords
from the Gower peninsula,
detailed from the womb
              to captain Industry
if they dont cop a packet this day
nor grow more wise.
Whereas C.S.M. Tyler was transferred from the West Kents
whose mother sang for him
at Mary-Cray
if he would fret she sang for lullaby:
              We'll go to the Baltic with Charlie Napier
she had that of great uncle Tyler
Eb Tyler, who'd got away with the Inkerman bonus.[12]

Every one of these, stood, separate, upright, above ground,
blinkt to the broad light
risen dry mouthed from the chalk
vivified from the Nullah without commotion
and to distinctly said words,
moved in open order and keeping admirable formation
and at the high-port position[13]
walking in the morning on the flat roof of the world
and some walked delicately
sensible of their particular judgment.

Each one bearing in his body the whole apprehension of that
innocent, on the day he saw his brother's votive smoke dif-
fuse and hang to soot the fields of holocaust; neither approved
nor ratified nor made acceptable but lighted to everlasting
partition.
Who under the green tree
had awareness of his dismembering, and deep-bowelled
damage; for whom the green tree bore scarlet memorial, and
herb and arborage waste.

Skin gone astrictive
          for fear gone out to meet half-way—
bare breast for—
to welcome—who gives a bugger for
the Dolorous Stroke.[14]

But sweet sister death has gone debauched today and stalks
on this high ground with strumpet confidence, makes no coy
veiling of her appetite but leers from you to me with all her
parts discovered.
     By one and one the line gaps, where her fancy will—how-
soever they may howl for their virginity
she holds them—who impinge less on space

sink limply to a heap
nourish a lesser category of being
like those other who fructify the land
like Tristram
Lamorak de Galis
Alisand le Orphelin
Beaumains who was youngest
or all of them in shaft-shade
at strait Thermopylae
or the sweet brothers Balin and Balan
embraced beneath their single monument.
    Jonathan my lovely one
on Gelboe mountain
and the young man Absalom.
White Hart transfixed in his dark lodge.
Peredur of steel arms
and he who with intention took grass of that field to be for
him the Species of Bread.
    Taillefer the maker,
and on the same day,
thirty thousand other ranks.
And in the country of Béarn—Oliver
and all the rest—so many without memento
beneath the tumuli on the high hills
and under the harvest places.[15]

But how intolerably bright the morning is where we who are
alive and remain, walk lifted up, carried forward by an effec-
tive word.

But red horses now—blare every trump without economy,
burn boat and sever every tie every held thing goes west and
tethering snapt, bolts unshot and brass doors flung wide and
you go forward, foot goes another step further.

The immediate foreground sheers up, tilts toward,
like an high wall falling.
There she breaches black perpendiculars
where the counter-barrage warms to the seventh power where
the Three Children walk under the fair morning
and the Twin Brother[16]
and the high grass soddens through your puttees
and dew asperges the freshly dead.

There doesn't seem a soul about yet surely we walk already
near his preserves; there goes old Dawes as large as life and
there is Lazarus Cohen like on field-days, he always would
have his entrenching-tool-blade-carrier hung low, jogging
on his fat arse.
　　They pass a quite ordinary message about keeping aligned
with No. 8.

You drop apprehensively—the sun gone out,
strange airs smite your body
and muck rains straight from heaven
and everlasting doors lift up for '02 Weavel.
　　You cant see anything but sheen on drifting particles and
you move forward in your private bright cloud like
one assumed
who is borne up by an exterior volition.

You stumble on a bunch of six with Sergeant Quilter getting
them out again to the proper interval, and when the chemical
thick air dispels you see briefly and with great clearness what
kind of a show this is.

The gentle slopes are green to remind you
of South English places, only far wider and flatter spread and

grooved and harrowed criss-cross whitely and the disturbed
subsoil heaped up albescent.

Across upon this undulated board of verdure chequered
bright
when you look to left and right
small, drab, bundled pawns severally make effort
moved in tenuous line
and if you looked behind—the next wave came slowly, as successive surfs creep in to dissipate on flat shore;
and to your front, stretched long laterally,
and receded deeply,
the dark wood.

And now the gradient runs more flatly toward the separate
scarred saplings, where they make fringe for the interior thicket
and you take notice.
   There between the thinning uprights
at the margin
straggle tangled oak and flayed sheeny beech-bole, and fragile
birch whose silver queenery is draggled and ungraced
and June shoots lopt
and fresh stalks bled
       runs the Jerry trench.
And cork-screw stapled trip-wire
to snare among the briars
and iron warp with bramble weft
with meadow-sweet and lady-smock
for a fair camouflage.

Mr. Jenkins half inclined his head to them—he walked just
barely in advance of his platoon and immediately to the left of
Private Ball.

   He makes the conventional sign
and there is the deeply inward effort of spent men who would
make response for him,
and take it at the double.
He sinks on one knee
and now on the other,
his upper body tilts in rigid inclination
this way and back;
weighted lanyard runs out to full tether,
                    swings like a pendulum
                    and the clock run down.
Lurched over, jerked iron saucer over tilted brow,
clampt unkindly over lip and chin
nor no ventaille to this darkening
                    and masked face lifts to grope the air
and so disconsolate;
enfeebled fingering at a paltry strap—
buckle holds,
holds him blind against the morning.
   Then stretch still where weeds pattern the chalk predella
—where it rises to his wire[17]—and Sergeant T. Quilter takes
over.

Sergeant Quilter is shouting his encouragements, you can almost hear him, he opens his mouth so wide.
   Sergeant Quilter breaks into double-time
and so do the remainder.
   You stumble in a place of tentacle
you seek a place made straight
you unreasonably blame the artillery
you stand waist-deep
you stand upright
you stretch out hands to pluck at Jerry wire as if it were bramble mesh.

No. 3 section inclined a little right where a sequence of
y.2's have done well their work of preparation and cratered
a plain passage. They bunch, a bewildered half dozen, like
sheep where the wall is tumbled—but high-perched Bran-
denburgers
from their leafy vantage-tops observe
that kind of folly:
nevertheless, you and one other walk alive before his parapets.

Yet a taut prehensile strand gets you at the instep, even so,
and sprawls you useless to the First Objective. But Private
Watcyn takes it with blameless technique, and even remem-
bers to halloo the official blasphemies.[18]

The inorganic earth where your body presses seems itself to pulse deep down with your heart's acceleration . . .
but you go on living, lying with your face bedded in neatly
folded, red-piped, greatcoat and yet no cold cleaving thing
drives in between expectant shoulder-blades, so you get
to your feet, and the sun-lit chalk is everywhere absorbing
fresh stains.

Dark gobbets stiffen skewered to revetment-hurdles and
dyed garments strung-up for a sign;
              but the sun shines also
on the living
and on Private Watcyn, who wears a strange look under his
iron brim, like a small child caught at some bravado in a garden, and old Dawes comes so queerly from the thing he saw
in the next bay but one.

But for all that it is relatively pleasant here under the first
trees and lying in good cover.

But Sergeant Quilter is already on the parados. He sorts
them out a bit
they are five of No. 1
six of No. 2

two of No. 3
four of No. 4
a lance-jack, and a corporal.
     So these nineteen deploy
between the rowan and the hazel,
go forward to the deeper shades.

And now all the wood-ways live with familiar faces and your
mate moves like Jack o' the Green: for this season's fertility
gone unpruned, & this year's renewing sap shot up fresh ten-
drils to cumber greenly the heaped decay of last fall, and no
forester to tend the paths, nor strike with axes to the root of
selected boles, nor had come Jacqueline to fill a pinafore with
may-thorn.
     But keepers who engineer new and powerful devices,
forewarned against this morning
prepared with booby-trap beneath
and platforms in the stronger branches
like main-top for an arbalestier,
precisely and competently advised and all in the know,
as to this hour
               when unicorns break cover
and come down
and foxes flee, whose warrens know the shock,
and birds complain in flight—for their nests fall like stars
               and all their airy world gone crazed
and the whole woodland rocks where these break their horns.

It was largely his machine guns in Acid Copse that did it, and
our own heavies firing by map reference, with all lines phut
and no reliable liaison.
     So you just lay where you were and shielded what you could
of your body.
     It slackened a little and they try short rushes and you find
yourself alone in a denseness of hazel-brush and body high

bramble and between the bright interstices and multifarious green-stuff, grey textile, scarlet-edged goes and comes—and there is another withdrawing-heel from the thicket.

His light stick-bomb winged above your thorn-bush, and aged oak-timbers shiver and leaves shower like thrown blossom for a conqueror.

You tug at rusted pin—

it gives unexpectedly and your fingers pressed to released flange.

You loose the thing into the underbrush.

Dark-faceted iron oval lobs heavily to fungus-cushioned dank, wobbles under low leaf to lie, near where the heel drew out just now; and tough root-fibres boomerang to top-most green filigree and earth clods flung disturb fresh fragile shoots that brush the sky.

You huddle closer to your mossy bed

you make yourself scarce

you scramble forward and pretend not to see,

but ruby drops from young beech-sprigs—

are bright your hands and face.

And the other one cries from the breaking-buckthorn.

He calls for Elsa, for Manuela

for the parish priest of Burkersdorf in Saxe Altenburg.

You grab his dropt stick-bomb as you go, but somehow you don't fancy it and anyway you forget how it works. You definitely like the coloured label on the handle,[19] you throw it to the tall wood-weeds.

So double detonations, back and fro like well-played-up-to service at a net, mark left and right the forcing of the groves.

But there where a small pathway winds and sun shafts play, a dozen of them walk toward, they come in file, their lifted arms like Jansenist Redeemers, who would save, at least, themselves.[20] Some come furtively who peer sideways, inquisitive of their captors, and one hides a face twisted for intolerable pain and one other casts about him, acutely, as who would take his opportunity, but for the most part they come as sleep-walkers whose bodies go unbidden of the mind, without malevolence, seeking only rest.

But the very young one
who walks apart
whose wide-lidded eyes monstrate immeasurable fatigue —
his greatcoat fits superbly at the waist and its tailored skirts have distinction; he comes to the salute for Mr. Trevor with more smartness than anything Mr. Trevor had imagined possible.

(and conscript-rookies in '17
got so bored with this tale.)
'89 Jones
'99 Thomas
             are detailed for escort.
They spring to it, very well pleased.

Perhaps they had forgotten his barrage down on the approaches, storming in the valley, reducing the reserves by one in three. Impaling this park on all sides but one, at which north gate his covering parties tactically disposed themselves:
             from digged-pits and chosen embushments
they could quite easily train dark muzzles
to fiery circuit
and run with flame stabs to and fro among
stammer a level traversing
and get a woeful cross-section on
stamen-twined and bruised pistilline
steel-shorn of style and ovary
leaf and blossoming
with flora-spangled khaki pelvises
and where rustling, where limbs thrust—
             from nurturing sun hidden,

late-flowering dog-rose spray let fly like bowyer's ash,
disturbed for the movement
for the pressing forward, bodies in the bower·
where adolescence walks the shrieking wood.

He watches where you lift a knee joint gingerly, to avoid low
obstacles,
with flexed articulation poked
from young leaves parted
        —and plug and splinter
shin and fibula
and twice-dye with crimson moistening
for draggled bloodwort and the madder sorrel.
    And covering every small outlet and possible sally-way and
playing old harry with any individual or concerted effort of
these to debouch or even get a dekko of his dispositions.

Now you looked about you for what next to do, or you fired
blindly among the trees and ventured a little further inward;
but already, diagonally to your front, they were coming back
in ones and twos.
    You wished you could see people you knew better than the
'C' Company man on your right or the bloke from 'A' on your
left, there were certainly a few of No. 8, but not a soul of
your own—which ever way.
    No mess-mates at call in cool interior aisles, where the
light came muted, filtered from high up traceries, varied a refracted lozenge-play on pale cheeks turned; on the bowels of
Sergeant Quilter,
and across feet that hasted
and awkward for anxiety,
        and behind your hurrying
you could hear his tripod's clank[21] nearer than just now.

But where four spreading beeches stood in line and the ground
shelved away about splayed-out roots to afford them cover
Dawes and Diamond Phelps
and the man from Rotherhíthe
with five more from 'D', and two H.Q. details, and two from
some other unit altogether.

And next to Diamond, and newly dead the lance-jack from
No. 5, and three besides, distinguished only in their variant
mutilation.

But for the better discipline of the living,
a green-gilled corporal,
returned to company last Wednesday
from some Corps sinecure,
who'd lost his new tin-hat, his mousey hair and pendulous
red ears like the grocery bloke at the Dry
said his sentences.
His words cut away smartly, with attention to the prescribed
form, so that when he said do this they bloody did it, for all
his back-area breeze-up high.[22]

For Christ knows he must persuade old sweats with more
than sewn-on chevrons or pocket his legatine prestige and lie
doggo.

But he'd got them into line at the prone, and loosing off
with economy; and he himself knelt at the further beech bole
to control their fire.

He gathered stragglers as they fell back and John Ball took
his position next to Private Hopkins and they filled the green
wood about them with their covering musketry; till Captain
Marlowe came all put out and withdrew them another forty
yards—then you had to assemble your entrenching-tool
parts and dig-in where you stood, for: Brigade will consoli-
date positions on line:—V, Y, O & K.[23]

And who's all this medley and where's Joe Pollock and he

saw Bobby Saunders get it early on and the Brigadier's up with
Aunty Bembridge and all with their Conduit Street bandboxed
shirtings, to flash beige and vermilion at the lapels' turn and
neat sartorial niceties down among the dead men and: It's only
right he should be with the boys the fire-eating old bastard.

Bring meats proper to great lords in harness and: I say Cal-
throp, have a bite of this perfectly good chocolate you can eat
the stuff with your beaver up, this Jackerie knows quite well
that organising brains must be adequately nourished
    But O Dear God and suffering Jesus
why dont they bring water from a well
rooty and bully for a man on live
and mollifying oil poured in
and hands to bind with gentleness.
    Fetch those quickly
whose linened bodies leaning over
with anti-toxic airs
would change your pillow-slip—
for the best part of them.
And potent words muttered, and
an anaesthetist's over-dose for gaped viscera.

But why is Father Larkin talking to the dead?

But where's Fatty and Smiler—and this Watcyn boasts he'd
seen the open land beyond the trees, with Jerry coming on in
mass—
and they've left Diamond between the beech boles
and old Dawes blaspheming quietly;
and there's John Hales with Wop Castello cross legged under
the sallies, preoccupied with dead lines—gibbering the formulae of their profession—
Wop defends the D III converted;[24]

and Bates without Coldpepper
digs like a Bunyan muck-raker for his weight of woe.

But it's no good you cant do it with these toy spades, you want axes, heavy iron for tough anchoring roots, tendoned deep down.

When someone brought up the Jerry picks it was better, and you did manage to make some impression. And the next one to you, where he bends to delve gets it in the middle body. Private Ball is not instructed, and how could you stay so fast a tide, it would be difficult with him screaming whenever you move him ever so little, let alone try with jack-knife to cut clear the hampering cloth.

The First Field Dressing is futile as frantic seaman's shift bunged to stoved bulwark, so soon the darking flood percolates and he dies in your arms.

And get back to that digging can't yer—
this aint a bloody Wake
for these dead, who soon will have their dead
for burial clods heaped over.
Nor time for halsing
nor to clip green wounds
nor weeping Maries bringing anointments
neither any word spoken
nor no decent nor appropriate sowing of this seed
nor remembrance of the harvesting
of the renascent cycle
and return
nor shaving of the head nor ritual incising for these *viriles* under each tree.

No one sings: Lully lully
for the mate whose blood runs down.[25]

PART 7

Corposant his signal flare
>   makes its slow parabola

where acorn hanging cross-trees tangle
and the leafy tops intersect.
And white faces lie,
 (like china saucers tilted run soiling stains half dry, when the
moon shines on a scullery-rack and Mr. and Mrs. Billington
are asleep upstairs and so's Vi—and any creak frightens you
or any twig moving).

And it's nearing dark when the trench is digged and they
brought forward R.E.s who methodically spaced their picket-irons and did their work back and fro, speak low—
cats-cradle tenuous gear.
You can hear their mauls hammering
under the oaks.
     And when they've done the job they file back carrying their
implements, and the covering Lewis team withdraws from out
in front and the water-party is up at last with half the bottles
punctured
and travellers' tales.
Stammer a tale stare-eyed of close shaves,
of outside on the open slope:
Carrying-parties,
runners who hasten singly,
burdened bearers walk with careful feet
to jolt him as little as possible,
bearers of burdens to and from
stumble oftener, notice the lessening light,
and feel their way with more sensitive feet—
you mustn't spill the precious fragments, for perhaps these
raw bones live.
     They can cover him again with skin—in their candid coats,
in their clinical shrines and parade the miraculi.

The blinded one with the artificial guts—his morbid neurosis retards the treatment, otherwise he's bonza—and will learn a handicraft.

Nothing is impossible nowadays my dear if only we can get the poor bleeder through the barrage and they take just as much trouble with the ordinary soldiers you know and essential-service academicians can match the natural hue and everything extraordinarily well.

Give them glass eyes to see
and synthetic spare parts to walk in the Triumphs, without anyone feeling awkward and O, O, O, its a lovely war[26] with poppies on the up-platform for a perpetual memorial of his body.

Lift gently Dai, gentleness befits his gun-shot wound in the lower bowel—go easy—easee at the slope—and mind him —wait for this one and
slippy—an' twelve inch an' all—beating up for his counter-attack and—that packet on the Aid-Post.

Lower you lower you — some old cows have malhanded little bleeders for a mother's son.

Lower you lower you prize Maria Hunt, an' gammy fingered upland Gamalin—down cantcher—low—hands away me ducky—down on hands on hands down and flattened belly and face pressed and curroodle mother earth
she's kind:
Pray her hide you in her deeps
she's only refuge against
this ferocious pursuer
terribly questing.
Maiden of the digged places
          let our cry come unto thee.
Mam, moder, mother of me

PART 7

Mother of Christ under the tree
reduce our dimensional vulnerability to the minimum—
cover the spines of us
let us creep back dark-bellied where he can't see
don't let it.
There, there, it can't, won't hurt—nothing
shall harm my beautiful.

But on its screaming passage
their numbers writ
and stout canvas tatters drop as if they'd salvoed grape to the
mizzen-sheets and the shaped ash grip[27] rocket-sticks out of
the evening sky right back by Bright Trench
and clots and a twisted clout
on the bowed back of the F.O.O. bent to his instrument.
. . . theirs . . . H.E. . . . fairly, fifty yards to my front
. . . he's bumping the Quadrangle . . . 2025 hours? —
thanks—nicely . . . X 29 b 2 5 . . . 10.5 cm. gun . . .
35 degrees left . . . he's definitely livening.

and then the next packet—and Major Knacksbull blames
the unresponsive wire.[28]

And linesmen go out from his presence to seek, and make
whole with adhesive tape, tweezer the copper with deft hands:
there's a bad break on the Bright Trench line—buzz us when
you're through.

And the storm rises higher
and all who do their business in the valley
do it quickly
and up in the night-shades
where death is closer packed
in the tangled avenues
fair Balder falleth everywhere
and thunder-besom breakings
bright the wood

and a Golden Bough for
Johnny and Jack
and blasted oaks for Jerry
and shrapnel the swift Jupiter for each expectant tree;
after what hypostases uniting:
withered limbs for the chosen
for the fore-chosen.[29]
Take care the black brush-fall
in the night-rides
where they deploy for the final objective.
    Dark baulks sundered, bear down,
beat down, ahurtle through the fractured growings green,
pile high an heaped diversity.
Brast, break, bough-break the backs of them,
every bone of the white wounded who wait patiently—
looking toward that hope:
for the feet of the carriers long coming
bringing palanquins
to spread worshipful beds for heroes.

You can hear him,
suppliant, under his bowery smother
but who can you get to lift him away
lift him away
a half-platoon can't.
How many mortal men
to bear the Acorn-Sprite—
She's got long Tom
and Major Lillywhite,[30]
        they're jelly-bags with the weight of it:
        and they'll Carry out Deth tomorrow.

There are indications that the enemy maintains his positions north-east of the central-ride. At 21.35 hrs[31] units

concerned will move forward and clear this area of his personnel. There will be adequate artillery support.

And now no view of him whether he makes a sally, no possibil-
ity of informed action nor certain knowing whether he gives
or turns to stand. No longer light of day on the quick and the
dead but blindfold beating the air and tentative step by step
deployment of the shades; grope in extended line of platoon
through nether glooms concentrically, trapes phantom flares,
warily circumambulate malignant miraged obstacles, walk
confidently into hard junk. Solid things dissolve, and vapours
ape substantiality.

You know the bough hangs low, by your bruised lips and the
smart to your cheek bone.
   When the shivered rowan fell
                 you couldn't hear the fall of it.
Barrage with counter-barrage shockt
deprive all several sounds of their identity,
   what dark convulsed cacophony
              conditions each disparity
and the trembling woods are vortex for the storm;
through which their bodies grope the mazy charnel-ways—
seek to distinguish men from walking trees and branchy
moving like a Birnam copse.
   You sensed him near you just now, but that's more like a
nettle to the touch; & on your left Joe Donkin walked, where
only weeds stir to the night-gusts if you feel with your hand.

All curbs for fog-walkers, stumble-stones and things set up
for the blind, jutments you meet suddenly, dark hidden ills,
lurkers who pounce, what takes you unawares, things thrust
from behind or upward, low purlins for high chambers, blocks
and hard-edged clobber to litter dark entries,

what rides the air
        as broom-stick horrors fly—
clout you suddenly, come on you softly, search to the liver,
like Garlon's truncheon that struck invisible.[32]

When they put up a flare, he saw many men's accoutrements
medleyed and strewn up so down and service jackets bearing
below the shoulder-numerals the peculiar sign of their battalions.
    And many of these shields he had seen knights bear before-
hand.
And the severed head of '72 Morgan,
its visage grins like the Cheshire cat
and full grimly.
    It fared under him as the earth had quaked—and the nose-
cap pared his heel leather.

Who's these thirty in black harness that you could see in the
last flash,
great limbed, and each helmed:
   if you could pass throughout them and beyond
—and fetch away the bloody cloth:
whether I live
whether I die.[33]
But which is front, which way's the way on and where's the
corporal and what's this crush and all this shoving you along,
and someone shouting rhetorically about remembering your
nationality—
    and Jesus Christ—they're coming through the floor,
endthwart and overlong:
Jerry's through on the flank . . . and: Beat it!—
that's what that one said as he ran past:
Bosches back in Strip Trench—it's a
monumental bollocks every time

and but we avoid wisely there is but death.[34]

Lance-Corporal Bains, sweating on the top line, reckoned he'd clicked a cushy get away; but Captain Cadwaladr holds the westward ride, & that's torn it for the dodger. Captain Cadwaladr is come to the breach full of familiar blasphemies. He wants the senior private[35]—the front is half-right and what whore's bastard gave the retire and: Through on the flank my arse.

   Captain Cadwaladr restores
the Excellent Disciplines of the Wars.

And then he might see sometime the battle was driven a bow draught from the castle and sometime it was at the gates of the castle.[36]

And so till midnight and into the ebb-time when the spirit slips lightly from sick men and when it's like no-man's-land between yesterday and tomorrow and material things are but barely integrated and loosely tacked together, at the hour Aunt Woodman died and Leslie's Uncle Bartholomew, and Miss Woolly and Mrs. Evans and anybody you ever heard of and all these here lying begin to die on both parties.

And after a while they again feel forward, and at this time the gunners seemed preoccupied, or to have mislaid their barrage-sheets, or not to be interested, or concerned with affairs of their own; and in the very core and navel of the wood there seemed a vacuum, if you stayed quite still, as though you'd come on ancient stillnesses in his most interior place. And high away and over, above the tree-roofing, indifferent to this harrowing of the woods, trundling projectiles intersect their arcs at the zenith—pass out of hearing, like freighters toil to gradients when you fret wakefully on beds and you guess far destinations.

Down in the under-croft, in the crypt of the wood, clammy drippings percolate—and wide-girth boled the eccentric colonnade, as perilous altar-house for a White Tower, and a cushy place to stuff and garnish and bid him keep him—or any nosy-bloody-Parker who would pry on the mysteries.

Aisle-ways bunged-up between these columns rising,
these long strangers,
under this vaulting stare upward,
for recumbent princes of his people.
Stone lords coiffed
long-skirted field-grey to straight fold
for a coat-armour
and for a cere-cloth, for men of renown:
Hardrada-corpse for Froggy sepulture.[37]

And here and there and huddled over, death-halsed to these, a Picton-five-feet-four paragon for the Line,[38] from Newcastle Emlyn or Talgarth in Brycheiniog, lying disordered like discarded garments or crumpled chin to shin-bone like a Lambourne find.

But you seek him alive from bushment and briar—
                              perhaps he's where the hornbeam spreads:
he finds you everywhere.
Where his fiery sickle garners you:
fanged-flash and darkt-fire thrring and thrrung athwart thdrill a Wimshurst pandemonium drill with dynamo druv staccato bark at you like Berthe Krupp's terrier bitch and rattlesnakes for bare legs; sweat you on the sudden like masher Bimp's back-firing No. 3 model for Granny Bodger at 1.30 a.m. rrattle a chatter you like a Vitus neurotic, harrow your vertebrae, bore your brain-pan before you can say Fanny—and comfortably over open sights:

the gentleman must be mowed.[39]

And to Private Ball it came as if a rigid beam of great weight
flailed about his calves, caught from behind by ballista-baulk
let fly or aft-beam slewed to clout gunnel-walker
below below below.

When golden vanities make about,[40]

you've got no legs to stand on.

He thought it disproportionate in its violence considering
the fragility of us.

The warm fluid percolates between his toes and his left boot
fills, as when you tread in a puddle—he crawled away in the
opposite direction.

It's difficult with the weight of the rifle.
Leave it—under the oak.
Leave it for a salvage-bloke
let it lie bruised for a monument
dispense the authenticated fragments to the faithful.
It's the thunder-besom for us
it's the bright bough borne
it's the tensioned yew for a Genoese jammed arbalest and a
scarlet square for a mounted *mareschal*, it's that county-mob
back to back. Majuba mountain and Mons Cherubim and
spreaded mats for Sydney Street East, and come to Bisley
for a Silver Dish. It's R.S.M. O'Grady says, it's the soldier's
best friend if you care for the working parts and let us be 'av-
ing those springs released smartly in Company billets on wet
forenoons and clickerty-click and one up the spout and you
men must really cultivate the habit of treating this weapon with
the very greatest care and there should be a healthy rivalry
among you—it should be a matter of very proper pride and
Marry it man! Marry it!
Cherish her, she's your very own.
Coax it man coax it—it's delicately and ingeniously made

183

—it's an instrument of precision—it costs us tax-payers, money—I want you men to remember that.

Fondle it like a granny—talk to it—consider it as you would a friend—and when you ground these arms she's not a rooky's gas-pipe for greenhorns to tarnish.[41]

You've known her hot and cold.
You would choose her from among many.
You know her by her bias, and by her exact error at 300, and by the deep scar at the small, by the fair flaw in the grain, above the lower sling-swivel—
but leave it under the oak.

Slung so, it swings its full weight. With you going blindly on all paws, it slews its whole length, to hang at your bowed neck like the Mariner's white oblation.

You drag past the four bright stones at the turn of Wood Support.

It is not to be broken on the brown stone under the gracious tree.

It is not to be hidden under your failing body.

Slung so, it troubles your painful crawling like a fugitive's irons.

The trees are very high in the wan signal-beam, for whose slow gyration their wounded boughs seem as malignant limbs, manœuvring for advantage.

The trees of the wood beware each other
                    and under each a man sitting;
their seemly faces as carved in a sardonyx stone; as undiademed princes turn their gracious profiles in a hidden seal, so did these appear, under the changing light.

For that waning you would believe this flaxen head had for its broken pedestal these bent Silurian shoulders.

For the pale flares extinction you don't know if under his close lids, his eye-balls watch you. You would say by the turn of steel at his wide brow he is not of our men where he leans with his open fist in Dai's bosom against the White Stone.[42]

Hung so about, you make between these your close escape.

The secret princes between the leaning trees have diadems given them.

Life the leveller hugs her impudent equality—she may proceed at once to less discriminating zones.

The Queen of the Woods has cut bright boughs of various flowering.

These knew her influential eyes. Her awarding hands can pluck for each their fragile prize.

She speaks to them according to precedence. She knows what's due to this elect society. She can choose twelve gentle-men. She knows who is most lord between the high trees and on the open down.

Some she gives white berries
        some she gives brown
Emil has a curious crown it's
        made of golden saxifrage.
Fatty wears sweet-briar,
he will reign with her for a thousand years.

For Balder she reaches high to fetch his.

Ulrich smiles for his myrtle wand.

That swine Lillywhite has daisies to his chain—you'd hardly credit it.

She plaits torques of equal splendour for Mr. Jenkins and Billy Crower.

Hansel with Gronwy share dog-violets for a palm, where they lie in serious embrace beneath the twisted tripod.

Siôn gets St. John's Wort—that's fair enough.

Dai Great-coat, she can't find him anywhere—she calls both high and low, she had a very special one for him.[43]

Among this July noblesse she is mindful of December wood —when the trees of the forest beat against each other because of him.

She carries to Aneirin-in-the-nullah a rowan sprig, for the glory of Guenedota.[44] You couldn't hear what she said to him, because she was careful for the Disciplines of the Wars.

At the gate of the wood you try a last adjustment, but slung so, it's an impediment, it's of detriment to your hopes, you had best be rid of it—the sagging webbing and all and what's left of your two fifty — but it were wise to hold on to your mask.

You're clumsy in your feebleness, you implicate your tin-hat rim with the slack sling of it.

Let it lie for the dews to rust it, or ought you to decently cover the working parts.

Its dark barrel, where you leave it under the oak, reflects the solemn star that rises urgently from Cliff Trench.

It's a beautiful doll for us
it's the Last Reputable Arm.

But leave it—under the oak.
leave it for a Cook's tourist to the Devastated Areas and crawl as far as you can and wait for the bearers.[45]

Mrs. Willy Hartington has learned to draw sheets and so has Miss Melpomené; and on the south lawns,
men walk in red white and blue
under the cedars
and by every green tree
and beside comfortable waters.

PART 7

But why dont the bastards come—
Bearers!—stret-cher bear-errs!
or do they divide the spoils at the Aid-Post.[46]
    But how many men do you suppose could bear away a third
of us:
drag just a little further—he yet may counter-attack.

Lie still under the oak
next to the Jerry
and Sergeant Jerry Coke.
    The feet of the reserves going up tread level with your fore-
head; and no word for you; they whisper one with another;
pass on, inward;
these latest succours:
green Kimmerii to bear up the war.

Oeth and Annoeth's hosts they were
who in that night grew
younger men
younger striplings.[47]

The geste says this and the man who was on the field . . . and
who wrote the book . . . the man who does not know this
has not understood anything.[48]

NOTES

GENERAL NOTES

1. Title-page of Book, *Seinnyessit e gledyf*, etc. See note 4, General Notes, *Y Gododdin*.

2. Dedication, p. xvii. *in the covert and in the open.* See note 47, Part 7, 'Oeth and Annoeth'.

3. Prologue, p. xix. '*Evil betide me . . . could not rest.*' From the Mabinogi of *Branwen ferch Lyr.* See Guest, *The Mabinogion.*

4. Quotations on title-pages of each Part. From *Y Gododdin*, early Welsh epical poem attributed to Aneirin (6th century); commemorates raid of 300 Welsh of Gododdin (the territory of the Otadini located near the Firth of Forth) into English kingdom of Deira. Describes the ruin of this 300 in battle at Catraeth (perhaps Catterick in Yorks.). Three men alone escaped death including the poet, who laments his friends. 'Though they may have gone to Churches to do penance their march has for its goal the sure meeting place of death.' He uses most convincing images. 'He who holds a wolf's mane without a club in his hand must needs have a brilliant spirit within his raiment.' There seems an echo of the Empire in the lines I use for Part 1:

    'Men marched; they kept equal step. . . .

     Men marched, they had been nurtured together.'

Perhaps he had ancestral memories of the garrison at the Wall; of the changing guard of the hobnailed Roman infantry. What seems to be one of the most significant lines I have put on the title-page of this book:

    '*Seinnyessit e gledyf ym penn mameu.*'

    'His sword rang in mothers' heads.'

The whole poem has special interest for all of us of this Island because it is a monument of that time of obscurity when north Britain was still largely in Celtic possession and the memory of Rome yet potent; when the fate of the Island was as yet undecided. (In Wales, the memory was maintained of *Gwyr y Gogledd*, 'the men of the north'. The founders of certain Welsh princely families came from the district of the Tweed late in the 4th century). So that the choice of fragments of this poem as 'texts' is not altogether without point in that it connects us with a very ancient unity and mingling of races; with the Island as a corporate inheritance, with the remembrance of Rome as a European unity. The drunken 300 at Catraeth fell as representatives of the Island of Britain. The translations are by the late Prof. Edward Anwyl. See his essay *The Book of Aneirin*. Hon. Soc. of Cymmrodorion, Session 1909–10.

5. Pronounce all French place-names as in English.

6. In such words of Welsh derivation as I have used the accent falls on the penultimate syllable.

PART 1

1. Title. *The many men so beautiful.* Coleridge, *Ancient Mariner*, part iv, verse 4.
   Men marched . . . equal step. See General Notes, *Y Goddodin*.

2. *San Romano.* Cf. painting, 'Rout of San Romano'. Paolo Uccello (Nat. Gal.).

3. *gun-fire.* Tea served to troops before first parade. Rouse parade.

4. *wallahs.* Person pertaining to: e.g. staff-wallah; person addicted to: e.g. bun-wallah.

5. *wads.* Canteen sandwiches.

6. *march proper to them. The British Grenadiers* is the ceremonial march of all Grenadier and Fusilier Regiments.

7. *late in the second year.* That is to say in December 1915.

PART 2

1. Title. *Chambers go off, corporals stay.* Cf. *Henry V*, Act III, Sc. i (stage directions) and Sc. ii, line 2.
   On Tuesday . . . enamelled shields. See General Notes, *Y Goddodin*.

2. *butt-heel-irons*. Metal at butt end of rifle furnished with trap opening into recess (i.e. the 'butt-trap') in which are kept necessary cleaning material, oil-bottle, pull-through, rag. See text, Part 4, pp. 63-64.

3. *tiny hay-stalks . . . immediate necessity*. Short jackets made from the hide of sheep or goats or other beasts, were issued to the troops in the line against the cold. They were afterwards abandoned in favour of dressed leather ones, which, though far less fascinating, were less an abode for lice.

4. *private ditty-bag*. The habit of carrying personal property of any sort into the line, was, from time to time, suppressed by the authorities. I have confused memories of a story of how some unit marching into the line with sandbags containing odds and ends of all sorts, bundles of dry wood, improvised braziers, parcels from home, was met by the Brigade Staff and compelled to dump everything by the road side. As parts of kit had been thrown in with these personal belongings, some people arrived in the front line without essential articles of equipment.

5. *They'll feel . . . send it down boy*. Invocations commonly employed to hasten: (1) a shower of rain (for discomfort of staff or to stop parades); (2) any manifestation of Divine judgment on the authorities.
   Rend the middle air. Cf. Milton, *Hymn on the Morning of Christ's Nativity*, verse 17.

6. *dumping valises*. Has reference to dumping packs at Q.M. stores when Battalion moved into the trenches. This practice did not, I think, become general until early in 1916.

PART 3

1. Title. *Starlight order*. Gerard Manley Hopkins, *Bugler's First Communion*, verse 5:
   > 'March, kind comrade, abreast him,
   > Dress his days to a dexterous and starlight order.'
   Men went to Catraeth . . . the weak. See General Notes, *Y Gododdin*.

2. *Proceed . . . sings alone.* Cf. Good Friday Office (Rubrics), Roman Rite.

3. *from the small.* Small of butt of rifle.

4. *Square-pushing.* From square-pusher, i.e. masher. Term used of anyone of smart appearance when in 'walking-out' dress.

5. *The Wet.* The wet canteen.

6. *night-lines.* Lights used by artillerymen on which to lay gun for night action.

7. *wagon lines.* The horse-lines of an Artillery Unit, some way to rear of gun positions. In the narrative an artillery supply wagon, having delivered its goods at the Battery, is returning to its wagon lines for the night.

8. *Barbara . . . hate.* St. Barbara, the patroness of gunners.

9. *Jac-y-dandi.* Cf. Jack-a-Dandy in Surtees's *Mr. Sponge's Sporting Tour.* *Nos dawch.* Corruption of 'Nos da i chwi'—'goodnight to you'.

10. *little gate . . . that place.* Cf. Malory, book vi, ch. 15.

11. *Jimmy Grove.* In homage to 'Scarlet Town', cf. *Barbara Allen.*

12. *a colder place for my love to wander in.* Cf. English folk song, *The Low Low Lands of Holland.*
    the lengthening light . . . lands. My mother always says, in February, as a proper check to undue optimism:
    > 'As the light lengthens
    > So the cold strengthens.'

13. *festooned slack.* Hanging field telephone wire. See note 18 to p. 36, 'mind the wire'.
    gooseberries. Arrangement of barbed wire hoops, fastened together to form skeleton sphere, the barbs thrusting outward at every angle; usually constructed in trench, at leisure, by day, convenient and ready to handle by night. These could be easily thrown in among existing entanglements.
    picket-irons. Twisted iron stakes used in construction of wire defences.

14. *I want you to play with*
    and the stars as well. Cf. song:

'Loola loola loola loola Bye-bye,
I want the moon to play with
And the stars to run away with.
They'll come if you don't cry.'

15. *caved robbers . . . Maelor.* 'The Red-haired Bandits of Mawddwy'
are notorious in local tradition. Historically a band of outlaws
who troubled the authorities in mid-Wales in the sixteenth
century, about whom legend has accumulated. Perhaps they
have become identified with that idea of a mysterious (red?)
race lurking in fastnesses which I seem to have heard about
elsewhere.

green girls . . . Croix Barbée. I had in mind Coleridge's *Christabel*,
and associated her with a nice dog I once saw & a French girl in
a sand-bagged farm-building, off the la Bassée–Estaires road.

16. *the cowsons: they've banned 'em.* A complaint against the H.Q. ban
on that kind of woollen comforter which covers the ears.
These articles of clothing were considered not conducive to
general alertness.

17. *cushy.* Used of any easy time, or comfortable place; but primarily
of any sector where the enemy was inactive. Habitually used,
however, whatever the sector, by the relieved to the relief as
they passed each other in trench or on road. These coming
from and these going to the front line used almost a liturgy,
analogous to the seafaring 'Who are you pray' employed by
shipmasters hailing a passing boat. So used we to say: 'Who
are you', and the regiment would be named. And again we
would say: 'What's it like, mate', and the invariable reply,
even in the more turbulent areas, would come: 'Cushy, mate,
cushy'.

18. *mind the wire.* Field-telephone wires, which were a frequent impediment in trench or on roads by night. They ran in the most
unexpected fashion and at any height; and, when broken,
trailed and caught on any jutting thing, to the great misery of
hurrying men.

19. *in wiv the Coldstreams.* It was customary for any new unit going into
the trenches for the first time to be attached to more experi-
enced troops for instruction.

20. *shell-case swung*. Empty shell-cases were used as gongs to give gas-alarm. This practice developed into the establishment of Gas Posts and Gas Guards. It was the function of these guards to note the direction of wind, and weather conditions generally and to set up notice, reading; 'Gas Alert', if the conditions were favourable to the use of enemy gas. If gas was actually being put over on the front concerned, the gong was struck, rockets fired, and clappers sounded. False alarms were common, and this weapon, more than any other, created a nervous tension among all ranks. The suspicion of a gong-like sound on the air was often enough to set a whole sector beating brass unwarrantably.

21. *he's got a fixed rifle on the road*. He, him, his—used by us of the enemy at all times. Cf. Tolstoy, *Tales of Army Life*, 'The Raid', ch. x, footnote: '*He* is a collective noun by which soldiers indicate the enemy.' It was part of the picked rifleman's duty to observe carefully any vulnerable point in or behind enemy trenches (e.g. a latrine entrance, a gap in parapet or between walls, a juncture of paths, any place where men habitually moved, the approach to a stream or pump), and, having taken registering shots by day, to set up a rifle aligned and sighted (i.e. a fixed-rifle) so as to cause embarrassment and restrict movement during those hours which otherwise would have been made secure by the covering darkness. Such points were called 'unhealthy'.

22. *the cleft of the Rock . . . hill-country . . . bugger of a time ago*. I mean those caves and hill-shrines where, we are told, the Mystery of the Incarnation was anticipated, e.g. at Chartres; and cf. Luke i. 39: 'And Mary arose in those days, and went into the hill country with haste, into a city of Juda' (A.V.); and there is the association of the moon with the Mother of God.

23. *O.B.L*. 'Old British Line.' In sector here describe ''lapidated series of trenches vacated by us in a local advance wa ¬alled.

24. *The Disciplines of the Wars*. Cf., as in other places, Shakespea 's *Henry V*. Trench life brought that work pretty constantly to the mind.

25. *hills about Jerusalem*. Cf. Welsh Calvinistic Methodist hymn, the
    concluding verse of which begins: 'O fryniau Caersalem'.
    David of the White Stone. Cf. Welsh song: *Dafydd y Garreg Wen*.

26. *Gretchen Trench*. Name given on English trench maps to German front
    line trench a little to left of road here described, a continua-
    tion of Sandy and Sally Trenches (see text, Part 4, p. 98).
    All German trenches were named by us for convenience.

27. *They've served . . . flares*. Together with various 'traditional song'
    associations here, I had in mind '*Eddeva pulchra*' and Wace's
    'ladies of the land . . . some to seek their husbands, others
    their fathers'.

28. *This gate . . . whispering*. Cf. Chaucer, *Knight's Tale*. Description
    of the palace of Mars.

29. *hurdle-stake*. Stout upright of revetting hurdle. Revetment hurdles,
    or revetting frames, were used to face the earth wall of crumb-
    ling breastworks with wire-netting.

30. *china*. From 'china-plate', rhyming slang for 'mate'.

31. *Kitty Kitty . . . in the City*. Cf. music-hall song popular among
    Field-Telephonists: 'Kitty, Kitty, isn't it a pity in the City you
    work so hard with your 1, 2, 3, 4, 5, and 6, 7, 8 Gerrard.'

32. *They bend low . . . however so low*. This passage commemorates the
    peculiar virtues of Battalion Signallers. They were a group of
    men apart, of singular independence and resource. Excused
    fatigues, generally speaking, and envied by the ordinary pla-
    toon soldier. Accustomed as they were to lonely nocturnal
    searchings for broken telephone wires, they usually knew the
    geography of the trenches better than most of us. They tended
    to a certain clannishness and were suspected of using the mys-
    teries of their trade as a cloak for idling. They also had the
    reputation of procuring better rations than those served to the
    platoon and of knowing ways and means of procuring extra
    comforts — such as officers' whisky, spare blankets, etc. Al-
    ways, of course, consulted as to any likely new move or turn
    of events, because of their access to 'the wires'. In general
    there was legend surrounding them as a body. They were cer-
    tainly a corporation within the larger life of a Battalion. They

197

seemed to us rather as Ishmaelites to a dweller within the walls.

33. *fire-step*. Raised step in fire-bay about two feet high, formed out of front wall of trench; sometimes built up with layer of sand-bags, sometimes furnished with a duck-board. This last was a good method, it allowed for drainage and afforded a drier seat. The fire-step was the front-fighter's couch, bed-board, food-board, card-table, workman's bench, universal shelf, only raised surface on which to set a thing down, above water level. He stood upon it by night to watch the enemy. He sat upon it by day to watch him in a periscope. The nature, height, and repair of fire-steps was of great importance to the front-line soldier, especially before adequate dug-outs became custom-ary in all trenches.

34. *bay*. Fire-bay. The built-out divisions in run of fire-trench. Each bay was connected with the next by a few yards of straight trench. The proportions of this traversing, formed by bay and connecting trench, varied considerably and might be angled square, and exactly and carefully revetted, or be little more than a series of regularly spaced salients in a winding ditch.

35. *Johnson hole*. Large shell-hole, called after Jack Johnson. It is a term associated more with the earlier period of the war; later on one seldom heard it used. It had affinity with that habit of calling Ypres 'Wipers', the use of which by a new-comer might easily elicit: 'What do you know about Wipers—Eeps if you don't mind'. It was held by some that 'Wipers' was only proper in the mouth of a man out before the end of 1915, by others, that the user must have served at the first Battle of Ypres in 1914.

36. *like long-barrow sleepers . . . as Mac Óg sleeping*. In this passage I had in mind the persistent Celtic theme of armed sleepers under the mounds, whether they be the fer sídhe or the great Mac Og of Ireland, or Arthur sleeping in Craig-y-Ddinas or in Avalon or among the Eildons in Roxburghshire; or Owen of the Red Hand, or the Sleepers in Cumberland. Plutarch says of our islands: 'An Island in which Cronus is imprisoned with Briareus keeping guard over him as he sleeps; for as they put it, sleep is the bond of Cronus. They add that around him are

many deities, his henchmen and attendants' (Plutarch's *De Defectu Oraculorum*; see Rhys, *The Arthurian Legend*). It will be seen that the tumbled undulations and recesses, the static sentries, and the leaning arms that were the Forward Zone, called up easily this abiding myth of our people. Cf. also Blake's description of his picture, 'The Ancient Britons':

'In the last Battle of King Arthur, only Three Britons escaped; these were the Strongest Man, the Beautifullest Man, and the Ugliest Man; these three marched through the field unsubdued, as Gods, and the Sun of Britain set, but shall arise again with tenfold splendour when Arthur shall awake from sleep and resume his dominion over Earth and Ocean.

'. . . Arthur was the name for the Constellation of Arcturus, or Boötes, the Keeper of the North Pole. And all the fables of Arthur and his round table; of the warlike naked Britons; of Merlin; of Arthur's Conquest of the whole world; of his death or sleep, and promise to return again; of the Druid monuments or temples; of the pavement of Watling-street; of London Stone; of the Caverns in Cornwall, Wales, Derbyshire and Scotland; of the Giants of Ireland and Britain; of the elemental beings called by us by the general name of Fairies; of those three who escaped, namely Beauty, Strength, and Ugliness.' See *The Writings of William Blake*, Descriptive Catalogue. Compare with note 42, below, 'Pen Nant Govid'.

37. *starving as brass monkeys*. Cf. popular expression among soldiers: 'Enough to freeze the testicles off a brass monkey.'
Diawl! Welsh expletive: Devil, one deprived of light.

38. *dogs of Annwn glast*. According to Lady Guest, writing in the forties of the last century, these baleful animals were still heard by the peasants of Wales, riding the night sky. *Glast* is an obsolete word meaning, apparently, to bark a lot.

39. *parked*. From 'parky' =cold.

40. *fog-smoke wraith they cast a dismal sheen*. Cf. Coleridge, *Ancient Mariner*, part i, verses 13 and 18. This poem was much in my mind during the writing of Part 3.

41. *organisation in depth*. The German trench system as a whole was of greater depth from the front line to the rear defences, of

greater complexity and better builded than was our own. At least, that was my impression.

42. *Pen Nant Govid . . . night flares.* This whole passage has to do with the frozen regions of the Celtic underworld. At Pen Nant Govid sits that wintry hag, the black sorceress, the daughter of the white sorceress, mentioned in the *Kulhwch ac Olwen*. Again, the Welsh called the chill Caledonian wastes beyond The Wall 'the wild land of hell'. And that theme of the revolving tower of glass in Celtic myth I associate with intense cold and yet with lights shining.

The place of the eight gates where Arthur and his men went, like our Blessed Lord, to harrow hell.

'And before the door of Hell's gates lamps were burning,
  when we accompanied Arthur—a brilliant effort,
  seven alone did we return. . . .'

The poem attributed to Taliessin from which this fragment is taken is called *Preiddeu Annwn*—'The Harrowing of Hades'. In another place it says:

'Before him no one entered into it. . . .
  And at the harrying of Hades grievously did he sing. . . .
  Seven alone did we return. . . .'

and this theme repeats itself at each gate:

'Beyond the Glass Fort they had not seen Arthur's valour. Three score hundred stood on the wall: Hard it is to converse with the sentinel.'

Arthur's descent into Hades is also associated with an attempt to obtain the magic cauldron which would hold the drink of no coward.

We who know Arthur through Romance literature incline to think that the Norman-French genius has woven for us the majestic story of the Table and the Cup, from some meagre traditions associated with a Roman-British leader, who possibly existed historically as a sort of local *dux bellorum*. (Cf. Collingwood and Myres, *Roman Britain and the English Settlements*, ch. xix.) But there is evidence shining through considerable obscurity of a native identification far more solemn and significant than the Romancers dreamed of, and belonging to true, immemorial religion—an Arthur, not as in the bogus print of the seal mentioned in Caxton's preface to Malory: '*Patricius Arthurus*

Brittanniae, Galliae, Germaniae, Daciae, Imperator', but rather
an Arthur the Protector of the Land, the Leader, the Saviour,
the Lord of Order carrying a raid into the place of Chaos.

As C. S. Lewis says of the mediaeval romance makers and
their use of Celtic material: 'They have destroyed more magic
than they ever invented' (*The Allegory of Love*, p. 27).

43. *third foot for him*. Cf. ninth-century Welsh stanza: 'Mountain snow
is on the hill. The wind whistles over the tips of the ash. A
third foot to the aged is his staff' (Skene, *Four Ancient Books of
Wales*).

44. *little cauldron* and *Joni bach*. Cf. song, *Sospan Fach*, associated with
Rugby Football matches; often heard among Welsh troops in
France. The refrain runs:

> 'Sospan fach yn berwi ar y tan,
> Sospan fawr yn berwi ar y llawr.
> A'r gath wedi crafu Joni bach,'

which implies, I think, that the little saucepan is boiling on the
fire, the big saucepan on the floor, and pussy-cat has scratched
little Johnny. It is a song of pots, pans, billikins, fire, and a song
of calamitous happenings. Mary Ann has hurt her finger, the
scullion is not too well, the baby cries in its cradle—it also talks
of Dai who goes for a soldier. There is an English version that
introduces the words 'Old Fritz took away our only fry-pan'
—which lends it more recent associations. I am indebted to the
secretary of the Llanelly Rugby Football Club, who kindly provided me with a copy of this song. When I wrote the passage in
the text, I had only the memory of great and little pans, of little
Johnny, of the trench where I heard it sung, of the billikins on
duck-board braziers, of some half-remembered saying about
'To Gwenhwyvar the pot, to Arthur the pan' (that may be quite
inaccurate)—and how, in the Triads, one of the three things
necessary to an 'innate *boneddig*' is his cauldron.

45. *the efficacious word*. There was one expletive which, above any
other, was considered adequate to ease outraged susceptibilities.

46. *at 350 . . . its bed*. Has reference to adjustment of back-sight leaf
for firing at required range. The opposing trench lines were, at

this point, separated by approximately 300 – 350 yards. In other places the distance was very much less. Among the Givenchy craters the length of a cricket pitch, at the most, divided the combatants (see Part 5, p. 116).

Kinross teeth . . . sixty-three parts properly differentiated. Scotsmen seemed as ubiquitous among Musketry Instructors as they are among ships' engineers. There are 63 parts to the short Lee-Enfield rifle.

47. *Those broad-pinioned . . . white-tailed eagle.* Cf. the Anglo-Saxon poem, *The Battle of Brunanburh.*

where the sea wars against the river. Cf. Dafydd Benfras (thirteenth century), *Elegy to the Sons of Llywelyn the Great:* 'God has caused them to be hidden from us, where the troughs of the sea race, where the sea wars against the great river' (trans. J. Glyn Davies, Cymm. Soc. Transtns., 1912–13).

PART 4

1. Title. *King Pellam's Launde.* Cf. Malory, book ii, ch. 16.
   Like an home-reared . . . piled sods. See General Notes, *Y Gododdin.*

2. *So thus . . . comforted.* Malory, book xiii, ch. 19.

3. *stand-to* and *stand-down.* Shortly before daybreak all troops in the line stood in their appointed places, their rifles in their hands, or immediately convenient, with bayonets fixed, ready for any dawn action on the part of the enemy. When it was fully day and the dangerous half-light past, the order would come to 'stand-down and clean rifles'. This procedure was strict and binding anywhere in the forward zone, under any circumstances whatever. The same routine was observed at dusk. So that that hour occurring twice in the twenty-four, of 'stand-to', was one of peculiar significance and there was attaching to it a degree of solemnity, in that one was conscious that from the sea dunes to the mountains, everywhere, on the whole front the two opposing lines stood alertly, waiting any eventuality.

4. *trip-wire*. Low strand-wire at about middle shin height, set some way apart from main entanglement, and often hidden in the long grass.

5. *like robber-fire*. Cf. *Kulhwch ac Olwen*: 'As Kai and Bedwyr sat on a beacon carn on the summit of Plinlimmon, in the highest wind in the world, they looked around them, and saw a great smoke toward the south, which did not bend to the wind. Then said Kai: "By the hand of my friend, behold, yonder is the fire of a robber."'

6. *gauze* and *boiling water*. Fine wire gauze was used to clean rifle when fouled after firing. Officially scarce and only reluctantly allowed to the rank and file, who set great store by it and who would barter a packet of cigarettes for a small piece. It cleaned the bore effectively & quickly, but was said to wear the rifling if constantly employed—boiling water was to be preferred, but not always easily procurable. In any case, 'There's nothing like a bit of gauze' was certainly the common soldiers' maxim.

7. *four-by-two . . . weighted cords*. Slips of flannelette 4 in. wide cut in lengths of 2 in. from a roll—oiled and drawn through barrel on pull-through to clean bore.

8. *S.A.A.* Small Arms Ammunition. Ball-cartridge.

9. *noon-day hour . . . comes walking*. Cf. Ps. xc. 6, Vulgate (A.V. Ps. xci).

10. *ease springs*. Part of formula at rifle inspection parade.

11. *all a green-o*. Cf. song, *Green grow the Rushes-o*:
    'Two, two, the lily-white boys clothed all in green-o.'
    (For Christians, Our Lord and St. John Baptist.)

12. *queen's unreason . . . bough plucking*.
    for the queen's unreason. Cf. the madness of Launcelot because of Guenever's stupidity when he lay the second time with Elaine unwittingly, and by an enchantment: 'He lept out at a bay window and there with thorns was he all scratched in his visage and body; and so he ran forth he wist not whither, and was wild wood as ever was man; and so he ran two years, and never man might have grace to know him' (Malory, book xi, ch. 3). She earned well the epithet the Welsh attach to her: 'Gwenhwyvar the daughter of Gogyrvan the Giant, bad when little, worse when big.'

beat boys bush. Cf. Formula used by boys in Ireland on St. Stephen's
Day:

> We hunted the wren for Robin and Bobin
> We hunted the wren for Jack of the Can,
> We hunted the wren for Robin and Bobin,
> We hunted the wren for everyman.

Merlin in his madness. There is a tradition that Merlin (*Merlinus Syl-
vestris*) lost his reason because of the violence of the Battle of
Arderydd and sought the solitude of the woods. Cf. The *Vita
Merlini* poem, of Geoffrey of Monmouth.

like green barley. Cf. *Y Gododdin*: 'Princes falling like green barley
on the ground'.

Keep date . . . bough-plucking. Cf. *The Golden Bough*, passages on
the Priests of Nemi.

13. *draughtsman at Army*. Man employed as map-drawer at Army H.Q.
Each Army had a fixed territorial command. Corps and Divisions might be moved from one Army Area to another as required. 'Army' signified for the front-line soldier a place very
remote, static and desirable. One spoke of anyone 'going to
Army' as if they'd done with the war.

14. *two o'clock from the petrol tin*. Formula used in giving direction of object to be fired at; called the clock method.

15. *as swung . . . on the tree*. Cf. *Golden Bough*, Odin and the Upsala sac-
rifices.

> 'I know that I hung on the windy tree
> For nine whole nights,
> Wounded with the spear, dedicated to Odin,
> Myself to myself.'

(Quoted from the Icelandic poem, the *Volospa*.)

16. *whose own . . . grey war-band . . . made their dole*. The German
field-grey seemed to us more than a mere colour. It seemed
always to call up the grey wolf of Nordic literature. To watch
those grey shapes moving elusively among the bleached breast
works or emerging from between broken tree-stumps was a
sight to powerfully impress us and was suggestive to us of something of what is expressed in those lines from the *Ericksmal* which
Christopher Dawson quotes in his *Making of Europe*: 'It is not

surely known when the grey wolf shall come upon the seat of
the Gods.' It would be interesting to know what myth-con-
ception our own ochre coats and saucer hats suggested to our
antagonists.

17. *Es ist ein Ros' entsprungen.* Cf. German carol.
Casey Jones . . . in his hand. Cf. music-hall song, *Casey Jones*, words by
Lawrence Seibert, music by Eddie Newton of U.S.A.

18. *square-heads.* Term used of the Germans, not perhaps so commonly as 'Jerry'.

19. *universall Peace through Sea and Land.* Cf. Milton, *Hymn on the
Morning of Christ's Nativity*, verse 3.

20. *as any chorus-end . . . fears.* Cf. Browning's *Blougram*:
'A chorus-ending from Euripides
And that's enough for fifty hopes and fears.'
or els . . . Park. Cf. Milton, *Hymn on the Morning of Christ's Nativity*,
verse 8.

21. *Jamaica Level.* In Rotherhithe.

22. *Dai de la Cote male taile.* Cf. Malory, book ix, ch. 1.

23. *hessian coverings.* Hessian material, from which sandbags are made.
Empty sandbags were used for every conceivable purpose. They
were the universal covering. They were utilised as a wrapping
for food; for a protection to the working parts of a rifle, and
cover for bayonet against rust. The firm, smooth contour of a
steel-helmet was often deprived of its tell-tale brightness, and
of its significant shape, by means of a piece of stitched-on sackcloth. The sand bag could be cut open and cast over the shoulders against the weather or tied round the legs against the mud
or spread as a linen cloth on the fire-step for a meal, or used in
an extremity as a towel or dish-cloth; could be bound firmly as
an improvised bandage or sewn together as a shroud for the
dead. There remained the official use: they constituted, filled
with earth, the walls, ceiling and even the floor surface of half
our world.

24. *the A.S.C. . . . against them.* Cf. song, *Mademoiselle from Armentieres*, verse directed against the Army Service Corps:
'The A.S.C. have a jolly good time, parleyvoo, etc.'

25. *these sit in the wilderness . . . other daemon drawn to other.* cf. Leviticus xvi; and *Golden Bough*, under Scapegoats.

26. *find the lane.* Gaps made in our own wire to facilitate going out and coming in of raiding parties were called 'lanes'.

27. *they press forward . . . in their complaint.* By far the greater number of men smoked cigarettes rather than pipes, and those who did complained bitterly of the particular blend of ration tobacco. So that the issuing out of these things usually called for considerable tact on the part of the N.C.O. in charge, and strained the amiability of those among whom they were to be divided.

28. *Since they brought us . . . Abdullas out of this earth.* Cf. Numbers xx. 10.

29. *char.* Tea.

30. *Knife-rest stances.* Wooden contrivance so shaped, used as framework on which to hang wire entanglement. Characteristically employed to block roads or any place where a portable obstruction was required.

31. *slatters.* Layers or repairers of slats, i.e. the flat pieces of wood which, laid laterally on two parallel lengths of timber formed a floorboard about 18 in. wide, frequently on wooden supports, so that the space beneath formed a drain, leaving the raised duckboard track dry to walk upon. They were in constant need of repair. They would, in a water-logged trench, become detached and float upon or be submerged in the water, causing considerable inconvenience to any party negotiating the trench, especially by night.

32. *The Salient . . . somebody else's war.* The Ypres salient, 20 miles north of sector here described; always a troubled zone. Any sound of bombardment coming from the north was said to be 'up Ypres way'.

33. *Land and Water.* Periodical well known for articles on strategy, contributed by H. Belloc.

34. *Green for Intelligence.* Green gorget-patches (tabs) were worn by Staff Intelligence Officers.

35. *back at the Transport.* Transport Lines. A battalion in the trenches left its transport wagons, field kitchens, carpenters, snobs, Quartermaster, Q.M. Sergeants, in the Reserve Area, a few kilometres to the rear.

36. *Pekin . . . Namur.* Cf. battle honours of the 23rd Foot. See also p. 122.

37. *My fathers . . . in Helyon.* The long boast in these pages I associate with the boast of Taliessin at the court of Maelgwn: 'I was with my Lord in the highest sphere, on the fall of Lucifer into the depth of hell. I have borne a banner before Alexander, I know the names of the stars from north to south, etc.', and with the boast of Glewlwyd, Arthur's porter, on every first day of May: 'I was heretofore in Caer Se and Asse, in Sach and Salach, in Lotur and Fotor, I have been hitherto in India the great and India the lesser and I was in the battle of Dau Ynyr, when the twelve hostages were brought from Llychlyn, etc.'; and with the boast of the Englishman, Widsith: 'Widsith spoke, un - locked his store of words, he who of all men had wandered through most tribes and peoples throughout the earth. . . . He began then to speak many words . . . so are the singers of men destined to go wandering throughout many lands . . . till all departeth, life and light together: he gaineth glory, and hath under the heavens an honour which passeth not away' (trans. from R. W. Chambers, *Widsith*). I understand that there are similar boasts in other literatures. I was not altogether unmindful of the boast in John viii. 58.

Additional Notes to above passage.

A. *for Artaxerxes.* Cf. the following reported front-area conversation: 'He was carrying two full latrine-buckets. I said: "Hallo, Evan, you've got a pretty bloody job". He said: 'Bloody job, what do you mean?'' I said it wasn't the kind of work I was particu- larly keen on myself. He said: ''Bloody job — bloody job in - deed, the army of Artaxerxes was utterly destroyed for lack of sanitation.''

B. *Derfel Gatheren. Derfel Gadarn,* 'Derfel the Mighty', whose wonder - working effigy, mounted and in arms, stood in the church of Llanderfel in Merionethshire. One of the great foci of devo - tion in late mediaeval Wales. The Welsh, with engaging opti-

mism and local pride, put aside theological exactness and maintained that Derfel's suffrages could fetch souls from their proper place. In the iconoclasm under T. Cromwell this image was
used at Smithfield as fuel for the martyrdom of John Forest,
the Greenwich Franciscan. The English made this rhyme of
him:

> 'Davy Derfel Gatheren
> As sayeth the Welshmen
> Brought him outlawes out of hell
> Now is com with spear and shield
> For to bren in Smithfield
> For in Wales he may not dwell.'

I quote from memory, and may be inaccurate, but it explains
my use of the form 'Gatheren' in text.

C. *in the standing wheat . . . (. . . bodies darting)*. Cf. Caesar, *Gallic
War*, book iv, ch. 32; book v, ch. 17.

D. *And I the south air . . . Espaigne la bele*. Cf. *Chanson de Roland*, lines
58 and 59:

> 'Asez est mielz qu'il i perdent les testes,
> Que nus perduns clere Espaigne la bele.'

I used Mr. René Hague's translation.

E. *'62 Socrates . . . duck-board*. Cf. Plato's *Symposium* (Alcibiades' discourse).

F. *The adder in the little bush . . . victorious toil*. Cf. Malory, book xxi, 4.

G. *In ostium fluminis . . . Badon hill*. These are the twelve battles of
Arthur as given in Nennius's *Historia Brittonum*. Nennius says
that at the battle at Guinnion Fort Arthur bore the image of
Mary as his sign; and the *Annales Cambriae* records under the
year 516: 'Battle of Badon, in which Arthur carried the cross
of our Lord Jesus Christ 3 days and 3 nights on his shoulders,
and the Britons were victorious.'

H. *loricated legions*. In Welsh tradition the Roman armies were so
called; it was said that Arthur led 'loricated hosts'.

I. *Helen Camulodunum . . . Helen Argive*. This passage commemorates
Elen Luyddawg (Helen of the Hosts), who is the focus of
much obscure legend. At all events she is associated in some
way with wearers of the Imperial Purple; is supposed to be the
daughter of Coel Hên, the legendary founder of Colchester;
patroness of the 'army-paths': '& the men of the Island would

not have made these great roads save for her'. The leader of armies abroad—a director of men; quasi-historical—so she seems to be discerned, a majestic figure out of the shadows of the last ages in Roman Britain.

J. *Troy Novaunt.* Cf. William Dunbar's poem, *In Honour of the City of London:*

> 'Gladdith anon, thou lusty Troy Novaunt.'

See note 42 to p. 89, 'descent from Aeneas'.

K. *I saw the blessed head . . . grievous blow.* There is a fusion of themes here. The predominant and general idea, of the buried king to make fruitful, & to protect, the land—here especially with reference to the head of Brân the Blessed under the White Tower in London. The exhuming of that guardian head by Arthur, who would defend the Land by his own might alone. The repeated spoliation of the Island by means of foreign entanglements and expeditionary forces across the channel—a subject recurring in Welsh tradition, and reflecting, no doubt, the redisposition of troops in the late Roman age, to support the claims of rival candidates to the Purple, and to stem the increasing barbarian pressure at different frontiers. The part played by Agravaine toward the climax of the *Morte d'Arthur*. The insult given to Branwen by the Irish, which insult, characteristically caused trouble between the two Islands. See the *Mabinogi* of Branwen, and Lady Guest's notes to that story.

Supplementary Notes to above:

They learned . . . beneficent artisans. The motif employed is from Triad xcii of the third series. When I wrote this passage I was aware of the doubtful nature of my source, but was not fully informed as to its completely spurious character.

The Bear of the Island; The Island Dragon; The Bull of Battle; The War Duke; The Director of Toil. Titles attributable to Arthur.

Islands adjacent. i.e. Wight, Anglesey and Man. 'The Island of Britain and the three islands adjacent' is a phrase common in Welsh legend.

Keeper of Promises. Caswallawn. Cf. the legend of how he led an expedition into Gaul against the Romans to recover a princess called Flur. He is called 'one of the three faithful ones of the Island of Britain' in the Triads.

that Lord Agravaine. I use Agravaine as a type of the evil coun-
sellor, because his malice was powerful in bringing about the
final catastrophe of Camlann. I have not forgotten Mordred
nor Gawain; but I see Agravaine as that secondary, urging influence without which the evil thing might not have been
brought to fruition.

L. *The Dandy Xth . . . saw Him die.* The Xth Fretensis is, in Italian
legend, said to have furnished the escort party at the execu-
tion of Our Lord. It will also be remembered that the Stan-
dard Bearer of this Legion distinguished himself at the land-
ing of Caesar's first expedition into Kent (Caesar, *Commentaries*, book iv, ch. 25). So that it has in legend double
associations for us.

Crown and Mud-hook is another name for 'Crown and Anchor', a
game of chance.

terrible embroidery . . . apples ben ripe. Cf. poem, *Quia Amore
Langueo*, version given in *Ox. Bk. of Eng. V.*

M. *You ought to ask . . . roof-tree.* Cf. the Welsh *Percivale* story, *Peredur ap Evrawc*: 'Peredur, I greet thee not, seeing that thou dost
not merit it. Blind was fate in giving thee favour and fame.
When thou wast in the Court of the Lame King, and didst see
the youth bearing the streaming spear, from the points of which
were drops of blood . . . thou didst not enquire their meaning nor their cause. Hadst thou done so, the King would have
been restored to his health and his dominion in peace. Whereas from henceforth he will have to endure battles and con-
flicts and his knights will perish, and wives will be widowed,
and maidens will be left portionless, and all this is because of
thee.' See also Jessie Weston, *From Ritual to Romance*, ch. ii.

N. *I am . . . Helyon.* 'In the fields of Helyon there is a river called
Marah, the water of which Moses struck with his staff, and
made the waters sweet, so that Israel might drink. And even
in our time, it is said, venomous animals poison that water at
the setting sun, so that good animals cannot drink of it, but in
the morning, after sunrise, comes the Unicorn, and dips his
horn into the stream, driving the Venom from it, so that the
good animals can drink there during the day.' (*Itinerarium Joan-
nis de Hese.*)

38. *Where's that birthmark . . . fade away.* Cf. Hebrews vii. 3, and
soldiers' song, *Old Soldiers Never Die.*

39. **5.9.** Read: five nine, not five *point* nine. In the ranks we always spoke of five nines, four twos, ten fives, etc., when referring to calibre of shells. But I have heard exalted men speak carefully of 'a ten point five centimetre gun' or 'a hundred and five millimetre shell'.

40. *the Boar Trwyth . . . a rag of them.* The mysterious destroying beast which is the subject of much of the *Kulhwch* story. He and his brood seem to typify the wrath of the beasts of the earth—and his name stands in Celtic myth like the Behemoth of Job. All Arthur's hosts could not draw him 'with a hook'. As with Leviathan: 'Lay thine hand upon him, remember the battle, do no more.' Lewis Glyn Cothi, a fifteenth-century poet, says of someone: 'He would destroy the towns with wrath, wounds and violence; he would tear down all the towers, like the Twrch Trwyth.'

41. *like Ewein . . . water-course.* Cf. *Y Gododdin*. '. . . the downfall of privilege was his slaughter by the streamlet; it was Ewein's ingrained habit to follow the upward path of a water-course.'

42. *Seithenin . . . December wood.*
    Seithenin . . . stove in. Refers to tradition of the inundation of Cantref Gwaelod ruled over by Gwyddno, whose drunken dyke-warden, Seithenin, failed to attend to his duties.
    Sospan Fach. See Part 3, p. 53, and note 44, 'Joni bach'.
    descent from Aeneas . . . cooked histories. See the story in Geoffrey of Monmouth (Geoffrey Arthur), of how Aeneas, after the fall of Troy, journeyed to Italy (as in the *Aeneid*), how his grandson Brute eventually came to this island and founded the British Kingdom, with the New Troy, London, as its chief city, and how he is regarded as the father of the British race. See note 37, J, to p. 81, 'Troy Novaunt'.
    Twm Shon Catti. The story of Twm Shon Catti is a local version of that general theme: audacious-robber-become-able-magistrate-married-to-beautiful-heiress. He is associated with the Tregaron-Llandovery district. A very broad-sheet type of hero.
    Mawddwy secrecies. See Part 3, note 15 to p. 35, 'caved robbers.'
    ein llyw olaf. 'Our last ruler', the last Llywelyn. Killed on December 10th-11th, 1282 near Cefn-y-Bedd in the woods of Buelt; decapitated, his head crowned with ivy. A relic of the Cross

was found 'in his breeches pocket'. The greatest English poet of our own time has written:

> 'And sang within the bloody wood
> When Agamemnon cried aloud.'

If the song of birds accompanied Llywelyn's death cry, with that chorus-end, ended the last vestiges of what remained of that order of things which arose out of the Roman eclipse in this Island. 'Ein llyw olaf' is an appellation charged with much significance, if we care at all to consider ancient things come at last to their term. He belonged, already, before they pierced him, to the dead of Camlann. We venerate him, dead, between the winter oaks. His contemporary, Gruffydd ap yr Ynad Côch, sang of his death: 'The voice of Lamentation is heard in every place . . . the course of nature is changed . . . the trees of the forest furiously rush against each other.'

whose wounds they do bleed by day and by night in December wood. Cf. *The Corpus Christi Carol.*

43. *supports.* Area of second line of trenches in front system, usually a few hundred yards to rear of front line.

44. *gas-rattles.* Wooden clappers used to give gas alarm.

   Mrs. Thingumajig's . . . flappers. Properly called 'The Ayrton Fan.' Designed to disperse gas hanging in dugouts or trenches. Any simple invention appearing among the troops was attributed to female ingenuity.

   toffee-apples. English trench-mortar projectile, the shape of which suggested that name—also, if I remember rightly, yellow paint was used on some part of them—which would aid to the similarity.

   picket-maul. Heavy mallet for driving home stakes used in wire entanglements.

45. *Big Ship.* (1) Generic term for any cross-channel boat, conveying troops from France back to England. (2) Leave-boat. (3) That mythological, desired ship, which would, at the termination of hostilities, bring all expeditionary men, maimed or whole, home again. Here, these town-bred Tommies would seem to have the seed of a very potent mythological theme.

46. *They strengthened . . . the watcher.* Cf. Nehemiah iii and iv.

47. *red and green and white.* Coloured rockets used as a gas S.O.S.

PART 5

1. Title. *Squat Garlands for White Knights.* (1) Shrapnel helmets were issued to all ranks in the early months of 1916. (2) G. M. Hopkins, *Tom's Garland*:

    '. . . garlanded in squat and surly steel.'

    (3) Carroll's *Alice through the Looking Glass*, ch. viii.
    He has brought . . . floor-hide. See General Notes, *Y Gododdin*.

2. *we're drawing . . . Blackamoor delectations.* To understand this and some succeeding passages it should be remembered that at this period rumours were current of units being moved to other theatres of war — particularly the near East. Like civilians who 'saw the Russians' in trains at Clapham Junction so soldiers in France 'saw' consignments of pith helmets, khaki-drill shorts, and even mosquito nets and body belts.

3. *He shall die . . . bloody jaw.* Cf. song about the toreador, Alphonso. I cannot recollect its title.

4. *'major.* Sergeant-major.
    Minnies. German trench-mortar projectile; also used of the mortar itself, from *Minenwerfer*.
    swinger. One who swings the lead = a malingerer.

5. *O my.* Cf. song, *I don't want to be a Soldier*.
    over the foam . . . Big Ship. See Part 4, note 44 to p. 93.
    Big Willie's luvly daughter. We used to sing a variation of the song: *Where are the boys of the village tonight*, which seemed to suggest that the object of the British Expedition into France was to enjoy the charms of the Emperor's daughter.

6. *We don't want ham . . . roly-po—ly.* Cf. song, *I do like a nice mince-pie*.

7. *Aisne stove.* A make of French kitchen-stove.

8. *tawny tooth . . . bent wit.* Cf. Skelton. I cannot find the passage I had in mind.

9. *Fancy religions.* Any religious denomination other than C. of E.

10. *four-fold shrill call*. Refers to use of whistle in calling companies to parade.

11. *me goggles are torn*. A mask for the eyes against tear-gas. The talc was apt to get cracked.

12. *Divisional siren acknowledges*. The powerful *Klaxon* horn at Div. H.Q.

13. *clean fatigue*. Fatigue-dress: worn for any work and for certain specified parades, consisting of tunic and trousers without puttees, with neither equipment nor arms. Great coats might be carried or worn as occasion required. Normally the service cap was worn but sometimes the cap-comforter (woollen stocking cap) was allowed and the steel helmet sometimes ordered. Fatigue dress proper was not worn in the line. It is associated with back areas, camps, places of training and rest.

14. *brasses*. The brass slides by which the length of the braces and belt of webbing equipment was regulated.

15. *unexpended portion*. 'The unexpended portion of the day's rations', official description of food (to be carried by party working away from camp or billets) left over from the morning's issue.

16. *The Dry*. The Dry Canteen.

17. *Ravenhills*. Firm of Thames-side engineers.

18. *white mare at Ler-ven-tee in' 15*. It was rumoured in 1915 that peasants near Laventie signalled to the enemy by means of a white horse moving in field.

19. *bah mal fay*. In parts of Yorkshire, I am told, peasants swear by 'Old Mauffey'.

20. *winged-pigs*. From Flying Pig—a type of trench-mortar projectile.

21. *Jolly Tars*. The 'Our silent navy' of the journalists was a topic of frequent jest among the troops in France.

Tin fish. Slang for torpedo. It was suggested that a submarine missile would be useful in the waterlogged trenches in the la Bassée area.

The Islands. The isolated posts on the Festubert front were called so. They could be reached only by night over duck-board tracks in the open, and consisted of small built-up breast-works—often without any parados, in a surrounding country of watery flats. 'The Grouse-butts' was another name for such posts.

22. *Rooshun roller.* 'The Russian steam-roller', which, we were told, would flatten the Central Powers.

Montycats. Mont-des-Cats. Hill to west of, and equidistant from, Poperinghe and Bailleul, from which notabilities could be shown the battle-front.

23. *stone-ginger.* An absolute certainty.

24. *his concavities is sufficient.* Cf. *Henry V*, Act III, Sc. ii: '. . . the con-cavities of it is not sufficient; . . . is digt himself four yard under the countermines; by Cheshu, I think, a' will plow up all . . .'

25. *canonical wiseness . . . this flesh.* It is required of priests, that they say with their lips the words of the Divine Office, the eye alone is not sufficient; a rule indicative of the Church's instinct as to the efficacy of bodily acts.

26. *Why cant the limbers carry the packs.* This was a perennial question during a Battalion move.

their blokes' valises. Batmen referred to those officers who employed them as 'my bloke'.

ox-blood kid. An officer's servant is here referred to—ox-blood polish was used for cleaning Sam Browne belts, etc.

pox doctor's clerk. Medical officer's orderly.

chitties. Cooks.

specialist details. Men detailed for specified job; e.g. sniping, bomb-ing, signalling.

chlorination Daniel. Used in text of man in charge of Battalion water-cart in which the chlorinated drinking-water was carried.

Old Man's water. The Commanding Officer's shaving water.

27. *dark ribbon.* The dark blue and red of the Distinguished Conduct Medal.

his longe ladel. Cf. Chaucer, *Knight's Tale*:
'The cook y-scalded for al his longe ladel.'

the worshipful . . . broth wallah. Cf. Malory, book vii, ch. 2.

28. *M.D. with broken blisters.* The particular circumstances described in text of consecutive days of rapid marching, following suddenly upon the cramped life in waterlogged trenches brought large numbers to the medical officer with crippled feet.

29. *withered are . . . stars frighted.* Cf. *Richard II*, Act II, Sc. iv.
    Dai Davies and the Sibyl . . . wave for sure. Cf. the *Dies Irae*: '. . . teste David cum Sibylla'.

30. *Albuhera, Oudenarde, Malplaquet, Minden.* Four of the Battle Honours of the 23rd Regiment of Foot. See also Part 4, p. 79.
    hound's coat mired. The White Hound as an armorial bearing is associated with North Wales.
    white mane tangled. Cf. Regimental Arms 23rd Foot: 'In the first and fourth corners the rising sun, in the second corner the Red Dragon, in the third corner the White Horse.'

31. *states.* Ration, etc., states. Reports concerning approximate numerical strength available for duties, or affecting supplies. These tended to get increasingly complicated.

32. *drum-fire.* Used of very heavy and continuous artillery-fire, but more properly of that tremendous & sustained concentration when that cadence, characteristic of a normally heavy bombardment flattened out into a faster and faster rhythm until no pulse at all was discernible, but only a kind of static violence—usually presaging infantry action. Indeed, any inflection in that level frenzy was taken as a signal of immediate attack.

33. *F.O.* Fighting order. Order of dress worn in an attack, indeed, normally in the front line.

34. *Old Johnny Fairplay . . . Mud-hook.* Formula used in *Crown and Anchor*, a game of chance.

35. *wives have puddings and pies.* Cf. words associated with bugle-call for 'Officers' Mess':

    > 'Officers' wives have puddings and pies
    > And sergeants' wives have skilly,
    > And soldiers' wives have sweet etc.'

36. *paper, pinned . . . verboten.* The pump-water in French farm-yards was very frequently put out of bounds by the medical officer.

37. *Runner Herne . . . windy plains . . . those deep-bosomed . . . the confeder-*

ates, brother. I had in mind Borrow's gipsy family and how runners shared that Ishmaelitish quality with the Signallers, mentioned in Part 3, note 34, 'they bend low'; and cf. Tennyson,
Ulysses:

> 'Far on the ringing plains of windy Troy';

and again, Borrow's gipsy's:

> 'Wind on the heath, brother'.

38. *and the selected ones . . . (. . . in the Companies)*. A friend tells me that
this does not easily yield its meaning. It refers to the Battalion
Bombers, who were, along with other 'Specialists', suspected
of getting better food than that issued to ordinary riflemen 'in
the Companies'.

medium T.M.s. Trench mortar detachments were classified: light,
medium, heavy.

rise and shine. Cf. formula for rousing sleeping men, which, compared with the more usual 'Show a leg', seemed to have almost
the quality of the monastic *Benedicamus Domino*.

Stokes people. Stokes-gun section.

39. *Where's the Sergeant-Major, I know where he is*. Cf. soldiers' verse:

> 'Where's the Sergeant-Major?
> I know where he is,
> I know where he is,
> I know where he is.
> Where's the Sergeant-Major?
> I know where he is,
> Down in his deep dug-out.'

(Accent on 'out'.)

General Weston's pure gold. General Sir Aylmer Hunter-Weston was
reported to have said 'The N.C.O.s of the British Army are
pure gold.'

Hur and that other . . . simply fades away. Cf. Exodus xvii. 12.

40. *affixing the mark at T. Atkins, etc*. Cf. form of will in soldier's Pocket Book.

mountings are much older Sonny boy. Cf. song:

> 'With thy musket on thy shoulder,
> Ere the mountains are much older
> Thou shalt tell who art the bolder,
> Son of mine.'

Daddy Brock's bonus. 'Brock's Benefit', an annual firework display at the Crystal Palace.

41. *you come in stockinged-feet and go aways in motor-cars*. Formula in game of chance.

42. *he'll burn . . . cock-boat*. I have somewhere read a letter (which I associate with Sir Francis Drake) on the defeat of the Armada, boasting that the enemy had not so much as burned a sheep-cote or sunk a cock-boat.

43. *mother of rivers*. Plynlimmon mountain is so called, because there issue from her bosom many rivers.
    wasted Gwaelod. See Part 4, note 46, 'Seithennin'.

PART 6

1. Title. *Pavilions and captains of hundreds*. Malory, and Hist. Bks. of O.T.
   Men went . . . their marching. See General Notes, *Y Gododdin*.

2. *And bade him* . . . Malory, book i, ch. i.
   and laid a mighty siege about . . . Malory, book xxi, ch. 2
   and great purveyance . . . Malory, book xx, ch. 12.

3. *The Alexandra*. The Alexandra Palace, Tottenham.

4. *So on the morn* . . . Malory, book x, ch. 29.

5. *construction of bivvy*. Waterproof ground-sheets were used to construct shelters in which to bivouac. It was customary for two or three men to lace together their ground-sheets and share the protection afforded. A low shelter, triangular in section, open at the end, long enough to lie down in, and supported by uprights, of whatever material was convenient, could, in this way, be contrived. If no supports of any sort were available the laced ground-sheets would simply be made to form a sleeping-bag.

6. *urgent or ordinary messages*. All messages were classified *urgent* or *ordinary*.

7. *mystery of theirs*. Engineers seemed always to be up to some job, about which, if questioned, they maintained an irritating reserve.

8. *sewn-on triangle . . . he sought*. Battalion identification marks were sewn on sleeve of tunic just below shoulder-numeral.

9. *He said there was a hell*. Various passages of Malory have influence here. Particularly book xx, ch. 1.
   Big-head . . . plain field. Important person. I have some disjointed memory of a cockney fragment, running: '. . . now the Big-heads will appear'.

10. *knocked-off*. Pinched, stolen.
    S.R.D. These initials were stamped on every ration rum-jar, and were interpreted by the troops: 'Service Rum Diluted'.
    diluted and far from home. Refers to statement frequently made by exasperated soldiers: 'Fed up, —d up and far from —ing home'.

11. *Esses Esses Bubble . . . Don Ac Ac Gees ; G, Esses, O, 1, 2 and 3 ; Ac Ac Q Emma Gees will fall on their dress swords*. South Sea Bubble, Deputy Assistant Adjutant General, General Staff Officer 1st, 2nd and 3rd grades, Acting Assistant Quartermaster General, in Signaller's Alphabet.

12. *Father Vaughan*. Eminent R.C. preacher; reputed to have urged greater zeal in the destruction of enemy personnel.
    Bull Ring . . . offensive spirit. The large training ground at Rouen, associated with intensive exercises of all kinds, particularly 'assault drill'. A paradise for Staff Instructors; detested by all front-fighters. The nature of the Ring is perhaps best described in the staff jargon elucidating the object of its curriculum, 'to foster the offensive spirit'.

13. *Divisional Rest*. A period when the entire Division was withdrawn from the line to reorganise and recuperate. It was attended by an access of discipline and physical training and the arrival of new drafts. To some temperaments 'Div. Rest' was not welcome.

14. *Woolly-Bears*. Very heavy German shrapnel, the burst of which gave off a dense blackish smoke, that sprawled the air in a thick rolling compact cloud.

15. *all the old . . . out there*. Cf. *Golden Bough*, under 'sympathetic magic'.
    O Clemens . . . guns amen. Cf. terminating lines of the *Salve Regina*.

PART 7

1. Title. *The five unmistakable marks*. Carroll's *Hunting of the Snark*, Fit the 2nd verse 15.
   Gododdin I demand . . . been found. See General Notes, *Y Gododdin*.

2. *Invenimus eum*. Cf. Ps. cxxxi. 6, Vulgate (A.V. cxxxii. 6).
   Matribus suis . . . suarum. Cf. Tenebrae for Good Friday, 2nd Lesson of 1st Nocturn. Lamentations ii. 12.

3. *Little Hours . . . intolerable*. The Canonical Hours of Prime, Terce, Sext and None. In the Little Office of the Blessed Virgin Mary (Dominican Rite), the psalms called *Songs of Degrees* are sung, including Ps. cxix, *Ad Dominum*, & Ps. cxxiii, *Nisi Quia Dominus* (A.V. Ps. cxx and Ps. cxxiv). Certain words in the Douay translation influenced this passage.

4. *Arthur's lap*. Cf. *Henry V*, Act II, Sc. iii.
   Olwen-trefoils. Cf. *Kulhwch ac Olwen*: 'Four white trefoils sprang up wherever she trod'.
   Yspaddaden Penkawr. The Giant task-setter in the *Kulhwch*. 'And Kaw of North Britain came and shaved his beard, skin, and flesh, clean to the very bone from ear to ear. "Art shaved, man?" said Kulhwch. "I am shaved," answered he.'
   Twrch Trwyth. See Part 4, note 40 to p. 86.
   Catraeth. See note to *Y Gododdin*, p. 191.
   seaboard-down, by Salisbury. Refers to Battle of Camlann. Malory, book xxi, ch. 3.

5. *Responde mihi*. Cf. Dominican Little Office of the Blessed Virgin Mary. Office of the Dead, 2nd Nocturn, Lesson IV (Job xiii. 22 to end of chapter).

6. *The Holloway*. The Holloway Empire Music Hall.

7. *O blow fall out the Officers*. To hear the bugle sound 'Fall out the Officers' was welcome to men on a wet day doing field exercises. It connoted the break off of operations.
   King's Birthday. A holiday for H.M. Forces—after the ceremonial parade.

8. *or you read it . . . in the Garden*. Cf. the Gospels (narrative of the Agony and of the Betrayal).

9. *china-plate.* See Part 3, note 30 to p. 47.

10. *Greenland Stairs.* In Rotherhithe.

11. *bis batty.* Interchangeable with 'china' (see Part 3, note 30 to p. 47) but more definitely used of a most intimate companion. Jonathan was certainly David's 'batty'.

12. *Mary-Cray.* Kentish village on outskirts of London.
    We'll go to the Baltic . . . Inkerman Bonus. Popular song from the period of Napier's Russian expedition:
    'We'll go to the Baltic with Charlie Napier
    And help him to govern the Great Russian Bear.'
    It is the first song I can remember my mother singing me.

13. *the high-port position.* Regulation position at which to hold rifle, with bayonet fixed, when moving toward the enemy. It was held high and slantingly across the body.

14. *Each one . . . and arborage waste . . . Dolorous Stroke.* Cf. Genesis iv; Malory, book xvii, ch. 5; Canon of the Mass, Prayer, 'Quam Oblationem', and Malory, book ii, ch. 15.

15. *shaft-shade.* Cf. Herodotus, book vii, *Polymnia*, Dieneces' speech.
    sweet brothers . . . monument. Cf. Malory, book ii, ch. 19.
    White Hart transfixed. Cf. *Richard II*, Act v, Sc. vi.
    Peredur of steel arms. Peredur. The *Percivale* of the romances called 'of steel arms' in the Triads, and by the Gododdin poet: 'Peredur with arms of steel . . .' (he commemorates other warriors, and proceeds) '. . . though men might have slain them, they too were slayers, none returned to their homes.'
    with intention . . . Species of Bread. In some battle of the Welsh, all reference to which escapes me, a whole army ate grass in token of the Body of the Lord. Also somewhere in the Malory, a single knight feeling himself at the point of death makes this same act.
    Taillefer . . . other ranks. Cf. Wace, *Roman de Rou*: 'Then Taillefer, who sang right well, rode before the duke singing of Carlemaine and of Rollant, of Oliver and the vassals who died at Renchevals.'
    country of Béarn . . . harvest places. Not that Roncesvalles is in the Béarn country, but I associate it with Béarn because, once,

looking from a window in Salies-de-Béarn I could see a gap in the hills, which my hostess told me was indeed the pass where Roland fell.

16. *seventh power . . . Three Children . . . Twin Brother.* Cf. Book of Daniel, ch. iii. Here I identify 'The Great Twin Brethren' at the battle of Lake Regillus with the Second Person of the Blessed Trinity —who walked with the Three Children in the fiery furnace.

17. *chalk predella . . . his wire.* The approach to the German trenches here rose slightly, in low chalk ridges.

18. *halloo the official blasphemies.* Refers to instructions given in bayonet-fighting drill. Men were cautioned to look fiercely upon the enemy when engaging him and to shout some violent word— and to not spare his genitals. This attempt to stimulate an artificial hate by parade-ground Staff-Instruction was not popular among men fresh from actual contact with the enemy.

19. *coloured label on the handle.* I cannot recall what it was, either stamped or labelled on the handle of a German stick-bomb, but I know the sight of it gave me some kind of pleasure—just as one likes any foreign manufacture, I suppose.

20. *Jansenist Redeemers . . . themselves.* There are crucifixes attributed to the Jansenists with our Lord's arms stretched narrowly above the head indicative of their error concerning the exclusiveness of the redemptive act.

21. *tripod's clank.* The movement of a German machine gun was often recognisable by the clank of chain or of some metal on metal.

22. *green-gilled . . . breeze-up high.* This Corporal had been recently sent forward to join his company in the line, from a safe job at Army Corps H.Q.

23. *on line :—V, Y, O, & K.* Letters indicating on Operations Map position on which troops concerned would dig themselves in.

24. *D lll converted.* Type of Field Telephone.

25. *Lully lully . . . runs down.* Cf. poem:
> 'Lully lulley; lully lulley!
> The falcon hath borne my mate away!'

26. *O, O, O, it's a lovely war.* Cf. song, *O it's a lovely war.*

27. *canvas tatters drop . . . shaped ash grip.* The canvas fabric of stretcher. The grip of handles of stretcher.

28. *F.O.O. . . . unresponsive wire.* Forward Observation Officer. An artillery officer having been sent forward to observe effect of our own or enemy fire is reporting to his battery by Field Telephone.

29. *Fair Balder . . . fore-chosen.* Here I have associated, in a kind of way, shrapnel with the Thunder God and its effect on the trees of the wood and with the oak-tree as the especial vehicle of the God and with the Balder myth (see *Golden Bough*), and how any chosen thing suffers a kind of piercing and destruction. Cf. Roman Breviary at Sext for the Common of Our Lady, Versicle.

30. *How many mortal men . . . Major Lillywhite.* I mean that the oak spirit, the *Dryad*, in fact, took these men to herself in the falling tree.

31. *21.35 hrs.* To be said: two one three five hours (9.35 p.m.).

32. *Garlon's . . . invisible.* The knight Garlon who rides invisible, striking where he will, through the pages of the *Morte d'Arthur*.

33. *When . . . whether I die.* Cf. Malory, book iv, ch. 15 (Launcelot at the Chapel Perilous).

34. *and but we avoid wisely there is but death.* King Mark's counsel in the Malory.

35. *He wants the senior private.* In the event of all N.C.O.s being killed or wounded the senior private soldier takes over.

36. *And then . . . castle.* Malory, book x, ch. 29.

37. *Down in the under croft.* Mordred's siege of the Tower, and memories of the Norman chapel there and Gothic tombs in a dozen churches directed me here.

   Hardrada-corpse . . . sepulture. cf. the notorious jest of the *hus-carle* to Tostig the Earl about the body of Harold H. See *The Heimskringla* History of Harald Hardrade, section 91.

38. *Picton . . . Line.* General Picton was of the opinion that the ideal infantryman was a south Welshman, five feet four inches in height.

39. *The gentlemen must be mowed.* Cf. Somersetshire song: *John Barleycorn.*

40. *golden vanities make about.* Cf. song, *The Golden Vanity.*

41. *county-mob back to back.* The Gloucestershire Regiment, during an action near Alexandria, in 1801, about-turned their rear rank and engaged the enemy back to back.

   Sydney Street East. It is said that in 'The Battle of Sydney Street' under Mr. Churchill's Home Secretaryship mats were spread on the pavement for troops firing from the prone position.

   R.S.M. O'Grady says. Refers to mythological personage figuring in Army exercises, the precise describing of which would be tedious. Anyway these exercises were supposed to foster alertness in dull minds—and were a curious blend of the parlour game and military drill.

   soldier's best friend . . . greenhorns to tarnish. I have employed here only such ideas as were common to the form of speech affected by Instructors in Musketry.

42. *You drag past . . . against the White Stone.* Cf. *Chanson de Roland*, lines 2259-2396, which relate how Roland, knowing that death is near for him, would break his sword on the brown stone, but it will not break, and how among the heaps of dead an enemy watches him, and how he lies by the white stone & the stone of sardonyx, and hides his sword *Durendal* under his body and dies.

43. *Dai Great-coat . . . one for him.* See pp. 70 and 79.

44. *Among this July noblesse . . . of Guenedota.* The north-west parts of Wales. See Part 4, note 42, 'ein llyw olaf'.

45. *Cook's tourist to Devastated Areas . . . for the bearers.* This may appear to be an anachronism, but I remember in 1917 discussing with a friend the possibilities of tourist activity if peace ever came. I remember we went into details and wondered if the unexploded projectile lying near us would go up under a holiday-maker, and how people would stand to be photographed on our parapets. I recall feeling very angry about this, as you do if you think of strangers ever occupying a house you live in, and which has, for you, particular associations.

46. *divide the spoils at the Aid-Post.* The R.A.M.C. was suspected by dis-
gruntled men of the fighting units of purloining articles from
the kit of the wounded and the dead. Their regimental initials
were commonly interpreted: 'Rob All My Comrades'.

47. *Oeth and Annoeth's hosts . . . striplings.* Cf. Englyn 30 of the *Englynion
y Beddeu*, 'The Stanzas of the Graves'. See Rhys, *Origin of the
Englyn*, *Y Cymmrodor*, vol. xviii. Oeth and Annoeth's hosts oc-
cur in Welsh tradition as a mysterious body of troops that seem
to have some affinity with the Legions. They were said to 'fight
as well in the covert as in the open'. Cf. *The Iolo MSS*.

48. *The Geste says . . . anything.* Cf. *Chanson de Roland*, lines 2095–8:
'Co dit la geste e cil qui el camp fut,
[Li ber Gilie por qui Deus fait vertuz]
E fist la chartre [el muster de Loüm].
Ki tant ne set, ne l'ad prod entendut.'
I have used Mr. René Hague's translation.

ET VIDI...AGNUM STANTEM
TAMQUAM OCCISUM.

THE GOAT ON WHICH THE
LOT FELL LET HIM GO FOR
A SCAPEGOAT INTO THE
WILDERNESS.

WHAT IS THY BELOVED MORE
THAN ANOTHER BELOVED.

NON EST EI SPECIES NEQUE
DECOR ET VIDIMUS EUM ET
NON ERAT ASPECTUS.

ERIT AUTEM AGNUS ABSQUE
MACULA, MASCULUS ANNI-
CULUS.

THIS IS MY BELOVED AND
THIS IS MY FRIEND.

Apocalypse v, 6. Leviticus xvi, 10. Song of
Songs v, 9. Isaias liii, 2. Exodus xii, 5.
Song of Songs v, 16.